MANCHESTER
UNITED®

CHAMPIONS AGAIN!

First edition published in 2003

Copyright © Manchester United PLC 2003
Text and design copyright © Carlton Books Limited 2003

Manufactured and distributed by Manchester United Books
an imprint of Carlton Books Limited, 20 Mortimer Street,
London W1T 3JW

Published in association with Future Publishing and
UNITED, the official magazine of Manchester United

A CIP catalogue record for this book is available from the British Library

ISBN 0 233 00054 2

Edited by:	**Justyn Barnes & Aubrey Ganguly**
Design:	**David Hicks**
Photographs:	**All pictures by John Peters &**
	Matthew Peters/Manchester United FC,
	(except pages 10 and 14, Action Images)
Match reports:	**Steve Black, Barney Chilton,**
	Paul Davies, Tony Howard,
	Andy Mitten, John-Paul O'Neill,
	Sarah Shaddick, Rebecca Stephenson,
	Michael Storey
Statistics:	**Opta@PLANETFOOTBALL.com**
Commissioning editor:	**Martin Corteel**
Cover design:	**Mark Lloyd**
Production:	**Lisa French**

PRINTED IN GREAT BRITAIN

MANCHESTER UNITED®

CHAMPIONS AGAIN!

OFFICIAL CELEBRATION

CONTENTS

SIR ALEX FERGUSON

IT'S A FANTASTIC FEELING TO BE CHAMPIONS AGAIN AND I'M REALLY PROUD OF MY PLAYERS. THEY'VE SHOWN DETERMINATION, PERSEVERANCE AND ABILITY AND THESE ARE THE QUALITIES THAT HAVE WON IT FOR US.

TO COME FROM SO MANY POINTS behind and catch Arsenal on the line is one of our greatest achievements as we were chasing a terrific side. We never gave up and that is what gave us the title. Given the start to the season Arsenal had and the injuries we had to overcome, it has been very hard. I'm not surprised people had their doubts about us in mid-season. But I know the capabilities of this team and I knew the players could take a challenge.

Our form in the final weeks of the season was unbelievable. Four goals against Liverpool, six against Newcastle, two scored at Highbury, three against Blackburn Rovers,

was the derby defeat by Manchester City in November. You sometimes need losses like that to refocus you on the job in hand. It happened in 1996/97 when Newcastle hammered us 5–0 and then we lost 6–3 at Southampton the following week, but ended up winning the league by nine points. You sometimes need to have the question asked as to whether you're still hungry enough, and the team responded well so perhaps the defeat by Manchester City was good for us.

The whole squad have played their part in us winning the league. Obviously, Ruud was fantastic and probably the main difference

Queiroz as my new assistant last summer. He's done a superb job. He takes the initiative and his preparations for matches are great. But I'd like to express my gratitude to all the backroom staff – they've all been fantastic and played their part.

I must also mention how delighted I was by the FA Youth Cup triumph. You only have to see how many of the first team players attended the final to see how much they think of the youth team boys. It's a massive achievement for coaches Brian McClair, Francesco Filho and all the young lads. The victory created a great buzz around the place. The Youth Cup is part of Manchester United. We've won it more times than any other club and that's because we pay more attention to youth football than most clubs.

At senior level, now we've won the league again, we'll try and improve next year. We have to look forward all the time at this club. The big one now is to win the European Cup again. We've only won it only twice in our history and that's not good enough for a club of this stature.

I'm just glad I changed my mind and decided not to retire last year – it was probably the best decision I've ever made! This season has been so exciting and I can't wait for the challenges ahead. Come August, we'll be ready to go again.

"TO COME FROM SO MANY POINTS BEHIND AND WIN THE TITLE IS ONE OF OUR GREATEST ACHIEVEMENTS."

two down at Spurs, four against Charlton and another two at Goodison on the final day. What a run that is!

There were so many great moments over the season for us to look back on, but I'd have to say our 6–2 win at Newcastle really stands out. That was one of the best performances we've ever had. You get maybe half a dozen team performances in a lifetime where every player excels and that's what happened that day. Everyone clicked. St James Park is a tough place to go at the best of times, but to go up there and get that result after losing in Madrid was fantastic.

In complete contrast, another memorable result from the season

between us and Arsenal in the final stages. But I was particularly pleased with our defence, which is young and still has scope to improve. Players like Quinton Fortune, Phil Neville and Diego Forlan have also made crucial contributions at certain times, particularly in terms of performing well when asked to play out of their natural positions. For example, Quinton came here as a left midfielder and Phil is recognised as a full back, but they both had magnificent games for us in central midfield. Indeed, Phil's display in our 2–0 win over Arsenal was one of the best individual performances of the season.

One of the best decisions I've ever made was appointing Carlos

CHAPTER ONE

WE WANT OUR
TROPHY BACK!

MANCHESTER UNITED began 2002/03 with much to prove. While Arsenal stormed to a League and FA Cup Double the Reds had ended the previous season trophyless for the first time since 1998. There were suspicions that United's stars had lost the extra edge of hunger that had brought them a decade of success. But with a new coach Carlos Queiroz on board and the £29.1 million summer signing of World Cup star Rio Ferdinand, United fans were hopeful of a positive start to the new campaign...

Wednesday 14 August
ZALAEGERSZEG TE (A)
CHAMPIONS LEAGUE QUALIFIER

Saturday 17 August
WEST BROMWICH ALBION (H)
PREMIERSHIP

Friday 23 August
CHELSEA (A)
PREMIERSHIP

Tuesday 27 August
ZALAEGERSZEG TE (H)
CHAMPIONS LEAGUE QUALIFIER

Saturday 31 August
SUNDERLAND (A)
PREMIERSHIP

Tuesday 3 September
MIDDLESBROUGH (H)
PREMIERSHIP

Wednesday 11 September
BOLTON (H)
PREMIERSHIP

Saturday 14 September
LEEDS UNITED (A)
PREMIERSHIP

Wednesday 18 September
MACCABI HAIFA (H)
CHAMPIONS LEAGUE PHASE ONE

Saturday 21 September
TOTTENHAM HOTSPUR (H)
PREMIERSHIP

Tuesday 24 September
BAYER LEVERKUSEN (A)
CHAMPIONS LEAGUE PHASE ONE

Saturday 28 September
CHARLTON (A)
PREMIERSHIP

Zalaegerszeg TE KOPLAROVIC (90) **1**
Manchester United **0**

WED 14 AUG 2002 ◆ 7.45PM GMT ◆ NEP STADION ◆ ATT: 27,500 ◆ CL QUALIFIER 1 ◆ REF: W STARK ◆ ENTERTAINMENT: ●●○○○

THE TEAMS

ILIC

BABATI CSOKA URBAN BUDISA SZAMOSI

FARAGO LJUBOJEVIC VINCZE EGRESSY

KENESEI

VAN NISTELROOY ❼ SOLSKJAER ❺

GIGGS ❻ KEANE ❼ VERON ❻ BECKHAM ❼

SILVESTRE ❼ O'SHEA ❼ BLANC ❻ BROWN ❻

BARTHEZ ❻

United Subs P Neville ❻ for Brown (5 mins), Forlan ❻ for Solskjaer (80 mins),
ZTE Subs Molnar for Egressy (65 mins), Balog for Farago (74 mins), Koplarovic for Kenesei (83 mins)

MATCH STATS

ZALAEGERSZEG TE		MANCHESTER UNITED
44%	POSSESSION	56%
3	SHOTS ON TARGET	5
1	SHOTS OFF TARGET	7
5	CORNERS	8
20	FOULS CONCEDED	14
1	BOOKINGS	2
0	RED CARDS	0

United star man ★

Ole Gunnar Solskjaer Worked tirelessly

Calamity as Koplarovic strikes in the last minute

A taste of our own medicine

> "The romance of football can see a small team have a big day and in a way I'm pleased for them"
>
> SIR ALEX FERGUSON

ON A BUMPY PITCH AND IN BLUSTERY CONDITIONS UNITED'S SEASON GOT UNDERWAY IN UNTHINKABLE FASHION.

WE LOST TO A TEAM FEW OF US HAD heard of in a manner we usually enjoy inflicting on others.

So lowly regarded were United's first competitive opponents of the season that you could have been forgiven for thinking that their name was actually 'Hungarian Minnows'. Although this could have be down to the fact that few could even say their name, let alone tell you where they were from. Zalaegerszeg TE, or ZTE, were making their European bow having won their first domestic title last season. It was hardly the type of record to indicate that a shock was on the cards.

Scarcely surprising then that the pre-match talk had been of how many we'd win by, with the consensus being that anything less than three would be a bad result. Even the ZTE fans were of similar thought. It seemed they were just glad to be in Europe and weren't even entertaining the idea that they might win the game.

In the past Manchester United have made a habit of saving themselves with late goals, particularly in the Champions League. This time the shoe was on the other foot. After a match that United had dominated despite being well below par, the Reds were caught with a sucker punch. In injury time a cross-field ball drifted over the head of Phil Neville, who was then unable to cut out the subsequent cross from the by-line and ZTE's second half substitute, Bela Koplarovic, put the ball past

Roy Carroll. The Hungarians celebrated like they'd just won the whole competition and the travelling Reds stood in stunned silence.

The final whistle blew shortly afterwards and so begun laps of honour from the team, wild celebrations in the stands and much chanting of "Zalaegerszeg – zeg – zeg – zeg!" The 28,000 reduced capacity Nep Stadion in Budapest was filled with incredulous Hungarian joy, and a smattering of Mancunian misery.

As we drifted out of the stadium and back into the Budapest city centre, opposition fans, in a state of delirium, surrounded us. It brought back unwanted memories of the game against Bayer Leverkusen. Then, the main feeling had been one of deflation that we'd not made it to Glasgow for the final. This time we were deflated because we'd been humbled, or rather embarrassed, by an inferior team. **PD**

THE TEAMS

CARROLL **1**
BLANC **7**   O'SHEA **7**
P. NEVILLE **6**   BUTT **8**   SILVESTRE **7**
   KEANE **9**
BECKHAM **7**   VERON **7**
   GIGGS **6**
VAN NISTELROOY **7**

DICHIO   ROBERTS
JOHNSON   GREGAN
MCINNES
CLEMENT   BALIS
GILCHRIST   SIGURDSSON
MOORE
HOULT

United Subs Solskjaer **8** for Veron (59 mins), Scholes **7** for P Neville (71 mins), Forlan **6** for Silvestre (76 mins) **WBA Subs** Dobie for Dichio (61 mins), Marshall for Roberts (70 mins),

MATCH STATS

MANCHESTER UNITED		WBA
75%	POSSESSION	25%
9	SHOTS ON TARGET	3
7	SHOTS OFF TARGET	1
9	CORNERS	1
10	FOULS CONCEDED	13
1	BOOKINGS	1
0	RED CARDS	1

United star man ★

Roy Keane Bossed the midfield

Manchester United SOLSKJAER (79 MINS)   **1**
West Bromwich Albion   **0**

17 AUGUST 02 ◆ 3PM ◆ OLD TRAFFORD ◆ ATT: 67,645 ◆ FA PREMIERSHIP ◆ REF: S BENNETT ◆ ENTERTAINMENT: ●●●●○

Red centurion Ole receives the plaudits

Back in the old routine

THE FIRST HOME GAME OF THE SEASON IS A FAVOURITE. IT'S ABOUT SEEING THE PEOPLE YOU ONLY SEE AT HOME MATCHES FOR THE FIRST TIME IN MONTHS.

THEY'RE NOT CLOSE FRIENDS BUT they're mates all the same, people who share so many memories because of Manchester United. It's handshakes all round and time to catch up. So and so has got married, another has had a change of career and another has gone off travelling. It's one of the rare occasions that United isn't the main point of conversation and it makes you appreciate the community that exists among fans.

I'm sure it was the same for West Brom fans; only they had the extra bonus of it being their first game in England's top flight since 1986. Baggies fans were loud and proud. There wasn't a better way to start life in the Premiership than with a trip to Old Trafford and they savoured the moment, posing for photos by the Busby statue and taking their seats long before kick-off.

At 3pm United set about the task of the expected victory. The atmosphere was loud in the visitors' section – they even had the cheek to sing, "It's just like being in church". But the overall mood soured considerably when the West Brom supporters sang the Dambusters tune with their arms outstretched.

Unsurprisingly, United fans took it to be an offensive reference to the Munich air crash. However, West Brom fans had unintentionally shown their naivety by singing such a song because no offence was intended – they always sing it at games and it's got nothing to do with Munich.

> "Ole always assesses what is happening round the field and to score 100 goals is a fantastic achievement"
>
> SIR ALEX FERGUSON

This misunderstanding led to a one-sided hostility.

On the field, United created chances they didn't convert. Many were surprised to see just Van Nistelroy up front with Keane given an advanced midfield role behind. With the score still goalless after an hour, Ole Solskjaer was introduced. West Brom were soon down to ten men when McInnes was dismissed for a two-footed tackle but their defensive resolve wasn't broken. 4–5–1 soon became 2–5–3 when full-backs Silvestre and Phil Neville were sacrificed for Scholes and Forlan as United chased that elusive goal.

11 minutes from time, Solskjaer (who else?) got that goal, his 100th in a Manchester United shirt. His goal in the Camp Nou cemented his legend, but he habitually saves United and his popularity continues to rise. May this star shine brightly for a long time at Old Trafford. **AM**

Chelsea GALLAS (3 MINS), ZENDEN (45 MINS)
2

Manchester United BECKHAM (26 MINS), GIGGS (65)
2

FRI 23 AUGUST 02 ◆ 8PM ◆ STAMFORD BRIDGE ◆ ATT: 41,541 ◆ PREMIERSHIP ◆ REF: G POLL ◆ ENTERTAINMENT: ✪✪✪✪✪

2–2: Cudicini is floored by Giggsy's 100th United goal...

Now we're starting to play

BEING PROMOTED TO EDITOR OF THE OFFICIAL UNITED MAGAZINE HAS HAD ITS ADVANTAGES. THERE'S THE THREE GRAND PAYRISE (THAT'S PER YEAR NOT WEEK) FOR A START, NOT TO MENTION THE IMPRESSIVE BUSINESS CARDS (WELL, MY MATES ARE ALWAYS IMPRESSED WHEN THEY'RE DRUNK).

BUT THERE IS AN OCCUPATIONAL hazard: I'm now expected to sit in the press box rather than the stands.

The view from the former is often better, but there are just too many oversized egos (not to mention

RYAN GIGGS BECAME THE FIRST UNITED PLAYER OF THE SEASON TO HIT THE WOODWORK IN 2002/03

1

stomachs) for it to be an enjoyable experience. My trip to Stamford Bridge did little to renew my enthusiasm – particularly when I spent too long chatting to Paddy Crerand at half-time and had to squeeze between belly and writing bench to get back to my seat afterwards (if looks could kill…). But there are some things you just can't knock Chelsea for. After all, who else would lay on champagne and crudités for the press when they're in so much debt? Their fans must be tearing their hair out, and

how Ken Bates must thank God he doesn't have prawn sandwich critic Roy Keane on his books.

One person he won't have been thanking pre-match, however, was his goalkeeper Carlo Cudicini. His words may have been twisted, but bold pronouncements to the media ("The way United threw the league away last season was a disgrace") are never a good idea when you're about to play us.

We weren't impressed when they scored an early goal against us either – Gallas touching home Zenden's

... and the celebrations begin!

What the papers said...

'At a time when United's hunger for more trophies has been questioned, the recovery from Sir Alex Ferguson's men was a forthright response to their critics. After David Beckham's first-half strike came a beauty from Ryan Giggs and had Poll spotted the foul by Carlo Cudicini on Scholes, it might have been six points out of six for United.'
Matt Dickinson, The Times

Ryan's rescue

'It's going to be another red carpet ride of mixed emotions for Manchester United fans. One thing became crystal clear at Stamford Bridge last night – if they continue to defend like this they will end up with nothing again. United in attack can beat anyone. Defending they look like a bunch of schoolboys at times. Opponents clearly are no longer intimidated by United, simply because they know they will score against them.'
Brian Woolnough, Daily Star

free-kick. But the goal only sparked United into playing some of the best football we've seen so far this season. It was no surprise then when Mikael Silvestre's superb long-ball found David Beckham and he cut inside and scored a fantastic goal with his left foot.

Things didn't look good when Zenden fired home from the edge of the area just before half-time, but the second half was all United. Giggs equalised with his 100th goal for the Reds in the 66th minute – thanks again to the excellent Mikael Silvestre – and it was only luck that prevented us from taking all three points. Well, luck and referee Graham Poll, who denied Paul Scholes a blatant penalty.

Post-match the champagne continued to flow, and it tasted all the sweeter for knowing United are getting back to their best. **SS**

> "They deserved a penalty and didn't get it... luckily for us"
> JIMMY FLOYD HASSELBAINK

Manchester United
Zalaegerszeg TE

VAN NISTELROOY 2 (6, 76 (PEN) MINS),
BECKHAM (15 MINS), SCHOLES (21 MINS),
SOLSKJAER (84 MINS)

5
0

TUE 27 AUG 02 ◆ 8.10PM ◆ OLD TRAFFORD ◆ ATT: 66,814 ◆ CL QUALIFER 2 ◆ REF: CC BATISTA ◆ ENT: ✪✪✪✪✪

THE TEAMS

CARROLL ❼

P. NEVILLE ❻ FERDINAND ❽ BLANC ❽ SILVESTRE ❼

BECKHAM ❾ KEANE ❽ VERON ❼ GIGGS ❼

SCHOLES ❼

VAN NISTELROOY ❼

KENESEI

EGRESSY

VINCZE MOLNAR ▪ LJUBOJEVIC

SZAMOSI BUDISA URBAN CSOKA BABATI

ILIC ▪

United subs Solskjaer ❽ for Scholes (50), O'Shea ❼ for Ferdinand, Forlan ❼ for Beckham (72)

ZTE subs Farago for Ljubojevic (59), Balog for Vincze (64), Turi for Babati (75)

MATCH STATS

MANCHESTER UNITED		ZALAEGERSZEG TE
60%	POSSESSION	40%
9	SHOTS ON TARGET	1
8	SHOTS OFF TARGET	4
6	CORNERS	2
16	FOULS CONCEDED	13
1	BOOKINGS	1
0	RED CARDS	1

Guess who has just scored a speciality free-kick?

United star man ★

David Beckham Commitment and flair

Did you ever doubt them?

> "This club's history is built on great European nights, and now we can look forward to more"
>
> SIR ALEX FERGUSON

THE ODDS SOME OF THE MANCHESTER BOOKMAKERS WERE OFFERING FOR A ZALAEGERSZEG VICTORY SAID IT ALL...

NOT EVEN A NO-HOPER THROWN against Mike Tyson in his early years reached odds of 20–1 against, so any niggling doubts as to the ultimate outcome of this fixture should have been allayed well before Ruud's fine opening strike.

Urgency, some crisp passing, some 20 minutes gone and by now not even an away goal would have been good enough for the unlikely Hungarian heroes of a fortnight ago, as David Beckham smacked a second with a trademark free-kick and then Paul Scholes' dogged determination got another goal for the home side.

With Sir Alex Ferguson seemingly unworried about the result, Rio Ferdinand made his long awaited Old Trafford debut (the Boca Juniors friendly aside) and with the match in the bag, the frenzied home crowd participation that accompanied the first 20 minutes soon subsided as eyes turned to our expensive new recruit. He has no worries about winning us over however, and the 'oos' and 'aahs' that greeted his every touch were only once replaced with a gasp of shock, when a pass actually went astray!

When Rio finally left the field, replaced by John O'Shea, there was an air of satisfaction that he'd not only come through the game unscathed but also that he was being replaced by his ultimate centre-half partner. The two men will surely eventually provide the solidity at the back that the manager has been craving since the Pallister–Bruce axis.

Two late goals sealed a comfortable victory, but by the time Ruud van Nistelrooy slotted away his penalty the game had died as an exhibition of anything but 'keep out of trouble'. With Paul Scholes limping off, injuries to Nicky Butt and the persistent 'Keane op' tittle-tattle doing the rounds, these are worrying times for Ferguson and the backroom staff who so far haven't had the luxury of deciding who will play in midfield once the opening salvos of both European and domestic football action have been fired. Up front however, one thing is for sure: Ole Gunnar Solskjaer's strike from the bench yet again did much to get the collective heads of the crowd nodding towards our Norwegian superstar getting an extended run in the team alongside Van Nistelrooy. Surely it will happen, and hopefully sooner rather than later. **SB**

THE TEAMS

SORENSEN

WRIGHT   BJORKLUND   BABB   GRAY

PIPER   MCATEER   REYNA   BUTLER

PHILLIPS

FLO

VAN NISTELROOY ⑩   SOLSKJAER ⑩

GIGGS ⑦   KEANE ⑦ ■   VERON ⑧   BECKHAM ⑩

SILVESTRE ⑤   BLANC ⑦   FERDINAND ⑦   P NEVILLE ⑩

CARROLL ⑥

Sunderland Subs Quinn for Flo (79), Thirlwell for Piper (89) **United Subs** O'Shea ⑥ for Silvestre (26), Forlan ⑤ for P Neville (89)

MATCH STATS

SUNDERLAND		MANCHESTER UNITED
50%	POSSESSION	50%
5	SHOTS ON TARGET	6
6	SHOTS OFF TARGET	11
6	CORNERS	8
15	FOULS CONCEDED	16
1	BOOKINGS	2
0	RED CARDS	0

United star man ★

Seba Veron By a head from Roy Keane... who lost his.

Sunderland FLO (70 MINS) — 1
Manchester United GIGGS (7 MINS) — 1

SAT 31 AUGUST 02 ◆ 3PM ◆ STADIUM OF LIGHT ◆ ATT: 47,586 ◆ FA PREMIERSHIP ◆ REF: URIAH RENNIE ◆ ENTERTAINMENT: ●●●○○

"Excuse me Mr Rennie, I would just like a friendly chat with my old pal Jason..."

A dark day at the Stadium of Light

WITH LESS THAN A MINUTE OF THIS GAME REMAINING, ROY KEANE WAS MY CANDIDATE FOR MAN OF THE MATCH.

SEBA VERON HAD GIVEN AN impressively fluent performance alongside Keane but even his display couldn't match the contribution of United's skipper. He'd been by far the best player on the pitch.

Then everything changed: Keane; Elbow; McAteer; Red card.

Leaving the ground, nobody was in any doubt as to what would make the next day's newspaper headlines. It was the only topic of conversation. Some United fans were vehemently defending him, criticising the wind-up tactics of "that Scouse b*****d McAteer". Others were more despairing of the United captain, accusing him of

"another moment of madness". Among the supporters there were clearly two schools of thought developing; those who feel he deserves our continued support regardless of his actions and those who think he's fast becoming a liability to the team.

Keane's absence through injury and suspension will be keenly felt by the team. Our start to the season has been a mixed one, with lows like Zalaegerszeg away followed by highs like the return leg. We need our captain around, especially in games like this one at Sunderland.

Taking the lead after only seven minutes through Giggs was nothing less than the team deserved and looked like being the first of many goals for the Reds. For an hour the United midfield dominated play, stroking the ball around effortlessly with the home players having no choice but to chase shadows. But, as

> "You have clashes in football matches. I had one or two in my career and I think Roy Keane and Jason McAteer have. It usually blows over"
>
> PETER REID

the old football cliché goes, 'you've got to take your chances'. United failed to. The Black Cats grew in confidence and their equaliser through the otherwise ineffective debutant Tore Andre Flo came as no surprise to anyone in the ground. It was definitely a case of two points dropped.

But that seemed the least of our worries as we made our way home to Manchester. The radio phone-ins were making typically grim listening, the gist of the calls being, "I've not seen the game yet but Keane's an animal." Clearly, if the callers had their way the United captain would be hung, drawn and quartered. Which illustrates the problem Roy must face. He has a reputation that makes him a target and while he continues to have rushes of blood like the one in this game, that situation is only likely to worsen. Let's hope his lay-off will provide him with the necessary strength to handle the challenges ahead. **PD**

Manchester United
VAN NISTELROOY (PEN 28)

1

Middlesbrough

0

TUE 3 SEPTEMBER 02 ◆ 8PM ◆ OLD TRAFFORD ◆ ATT: 67,464 ◆ FA PREMIERSHIP ◆ REF: MIKE RILEY ◆ ENTERTAINMENT: ✪✪✪✪✪

Ruud celebrates his first goal in the 2002/03 Premiership

THE TEAMS

BARTHEZ 6

FERDINAND 8   BLANC 7

P NEVILLE 6   SILVESTRE 6

BUTT 6   VERON 6

BECKHAM 6   SCHOLES 6   GIGGS 6

VAN NISTELROOY 6

GREENING   JOB   MACCARONE   GEREMI

BOATENG

QUEDRUE   COOPER   EHIOGU   STOCKDALE

SOUTHGATE

SCHWARZER

United Subs Solskjaer 5 for Van Nistelrooy (71), Forlan 6 for Scholes (79), O'Shea 6 for Beckham (89)
Middlesbrough Subs Whelan for Quedrue (73), Marinelli for Maccarone

MATCH STATS

MANCHESTER UNITED		MIDDLESBROUGH
53%	POSSESSION	47%
2	SHOTS ON TARGET	2
9	SHOTS OFF TARGET	2
5	CORNERS	2
16	FOULS CONCEDED	14
1	BOOKINGS	2
0	RED CARDS	0

United star man ★

Rio Ferdinand Calm and tidy

A win without frills (or thrills)

> "We have three points but I think it's best to forget this game and move on"
>
> RUUD VAN NISTELROOY

THREE POINTS IN THE BAG, BUT YOU WOULDN'T HAVE THOUGHT IT. THE WORRIED, PENSIVE FACES SPORTED BY THE DEPARTING MASSES FROM OT SAID IT ALL.

THE SILENCE, PUNCTUATED ONLY BY the odd distant tirade, spoke volumes. This was not the free-flowing Manchester United we'd grown accustomed to of late.

With the furore surrounding Roy Keane, Middlesbrough had been almost forgotten. All the pre-match talk concerned the effect the skipper's hip operation would have on our already stuttering season, with fans all too aware of his enormous influence. In the 10 league games Keano missed last year we dropped 13 points, a record which cannot continue if we

are to be in contention on his return.

This perhaps wouldn't have been the preferred game with which to start the Keane-free period. Middlesbrough always seem to come and set out their stall to frustrate with some success, accentuated by ex-Red Steve McClaren's inside knowledge. With this in mind, there were a few raised eyebrows at the sight of Solskjaer warming the bench, leaving Ruud to fight a lone battle up front.

In a flat atmosphere, a narrow United struggled to break through the visitors' stubborn defence, and with Boro's reluctance to venture forward the first half became a low tempo affair, only really punctuated by the eventual telling moment of the game. Thankfully Mike Riley was one of only a few people who spotted Ehiogu's grasp for Van Nistelrooy's left arm as the Dutchman put his shot over and gave him another chance from the spot.

As we've come to expect, Ruud dispatched the penalty with minimum fuss, and looked mightily relieved to finally get off the mark in the league.

In the second half the crowd's pleas were answered as Solskjaer was given his chance for the last 20 minutes, but it was to replace rather than aid the toiling Van Nistelrooy and by then it seemed that even Roy Keane would've had trouble injecting any energy into what had long become a lacklustre affair.

Lacklustre or not, three points are three points and it was to the defence's credit that their concentration held firm to repel Middlesbrough's late rally. Last season this game may well have ended 1–1, but Rio Ferdinand is fast becoming the vocal force needed in defence. Two home league games and two clean sheets. Not too shabby... now for some goals! **RS**

THE TEAMS

BARTHEZ ⑥

FERDINAND ⑥   BLANC ⑥

P NEVILLE ⑥   BUTT ⑦   SILVESTRE ⑦

BECKHAM ⑧   VERON ⑥   GIGGS ⑥

VAN NISTELROOY ⑥   SOLSKJAER ⑥

RICKETTS

DJORKAEFF   PEDERSEN

GARDNER   NOLAN   FRANDSEN

CHARLTON   BARNESS

WHITLOW   BERGSSON

JAASKELAINEN

United Subs Forlan ⑦ for Veron (79)
Bolton Subs Warhurst for Djorkaeff (73), Holdsworth for Frandsen (87), Campo for Pedersen (89)

MATCH STATS

MANCHESTER UNITED		BOLTON WANDERERS
58%	POSSESSION	42%
7	SHOTS ON TARGET	2
10	SHOTS OFF TARGET	3
9	CORNERS	6
10	FOULS CONCEDED	13
1	BOOKINGS	2
0	RED CARDS	0

United star man ⭐

David Beckham Despite *that* mis-hit clearance...

Manchester United   0
Bolton Wanderers   1
NOLAN (76 MINS)

WED 11 SEPT 02 ◆ 8PM ◆ OLD TRAFFORD ◆ ATT: 67,623 ◆ FA BARCLAYCARD PREMIERSHIP ◆ REF: G.BARBER ◆ ENTERTAINMENT: ✪✪✪✪✪

Butt flies in to challenge Gardner

Stop press: Bolton win World Cup again!

WHILE I WASN'T SEEKING SICILIAN-STYLE RETRIBUTION FROM OLD TRAFFORD'S FOURTH COMPETITIVE FIXTURE OF THE SEASON, IF REVENGE IS TO BE A DISH BEST SERVED COLD, I'D NOW BEEN WAITING LONG ENOUGH FOR UNITED TO MAKE AMENDS FOR THAT HOME DEFEAT LAST SEASON.

SIR MATT BUSBY WAY WAS AWASH with pre-match optimism, as only an evening fixture and a few post-work pints can produce. Sadly, for the second year running, the game didn't conform to the script we'd wanted and expected. Bolton played their hearts out again, but a Manchester United attack currently lacking in confidence found themselves unable to strike through their ageing defence.

It would be less than 72 hours later, after defeat against Leeds United, that the press would sharpen their quills and suggest a crisis. But the worry here tonight was that our team that "always score" didn't again or create

any space or chances down the flanks. Frustration from all corners grew and the stereotypical bloke behind me didn't even need to be invented as he continuously griped: "This has a 0–0 draw written all over it".

While at times I couldn't see us breaking them down, I couldn't see them breaking us down either. It was going to take an individual error to allow them their opportunity, and David Beckham's missed clearance on the edge of the area was sadly just that. History was repeating itself and Bolton supporters were on the verge of celebrating another World Cup final win!

> "We take the glory and the bad times together. We're not blaming anyone"
> PHIL NEVILLE

It's ludicrous to make any sort of long-term judgements after five games, but West Bromwich Albion, Middlesbrough and Bolton Wanderers all seemed set on wanting to defend a 0–0 scoreline from start to finish. Not so long ago we'd have been celebrating the folly of their misguided approach within minutes of the start.

Seba Veron had produced some marvellous touches, including a one-two move that was quite simply world class. Yet this was followed by some sloppy mis-directed passes. But it was still a surprise to see him substituted late-on when his creative edge might have provided the opening we needed. The last five minutes saw a typical United bombardment. Barthez went forward like Schmeichel, Ole and Diego both nearly snatched a draw. It wasn't to be. The post-match gloom among fans contrasted sharply with pre-match optimism. But we'll bounce back from this. We have to. **BC**

Leeds United KEWELL (67 MINS)

Manchester United

1
0

SAT 14 SEPTEMBER 02 ◆ 12 NOON ◆ ELLAND ROAD ◆ ATT: 39,622 ◆ FA PREMIERSHIP ◆ REF: J WINTER ◆ ENTERTAINMENT: ◖◖◖◗◗

Tough times, but the Gaffer knows it's a marathon not a sprint

Another defeat, but no need to panic

A DECADE OR SO AGO THE LABOUR PARTY WAS UNELECTABLE. AS THE CONSERVATIVES WON ELECTIONS, EACH YEAR THE LABOUR PARTY CONFERENCE HELD INQUESTS INTO WHAT WAS WRONG – AND EACH YEAR THEY FAILED TO REALISE THAT 'WASHING THEIR DIRTY LINEN IN PUBLIC' WAS THE REASON.

THEIR POLICIES WEREN'T BAD, THE views they had weren't bad either, but the bickering and blaming made the opposite appear true. They suffered, and the radical changes being advocated led them further and further from power.

Manchester United FC is not in turmoil. It has not become a 'club in

crisis'. It has not finished its reign at the top of the game. While the press and supporters from other clubs revel in our 'demise', we must relax and look inwards to what made us strong in the first place – and that means no knee-jerk reactions and no recriminations. It means keeping things in-house and believing in our

players and our manager. It means not falling into the trap of ringing phone-ins and agreeing with the ludicrous mutterings that Fergie must go; that Veron is an appalling buy; that Keano has cost us dearly, and that Becks and co are long since past caring.

On Saturday we were without our heartbeat Roy Keane. We were without Paul Scholes, so often an inspiration and an almost indelibly etched name on the teamsheet. We were without Juan Sebastian Veron, a man ridiculed and chastised for

RUUD VAN NISTELROOY AND OLE SOLSKJAER MANAGED JUST TWO SHOTS ON TARGET BETWEEN THEM **2**

Viduka keeps Larry at bay

MATCH STATS

LEEDS UNITED		MANCHESTER UNITED
43%	POSSESSION	57%
3	SHOTS ON TARGET	5
6	SHOTS OFF TARGET	2
4	CORNERS	7
16	FOULS CONCEDED	13
2	BOOKINGS	1
0	RED CARDS	0

United star man ★

Rio Ferdinand Coped calmly with the Leeds' fans abuse

SHOTS	0
PASSES	53
PASS COMPLETION %	64%
TACKLES	5
TACKLE SUCCESS	100%
CLEARANCES	3
FOULS	0

doing nothing more than costing us a great deal of money in an over-inflated transfer market. But come on, anybody who has watched him closely knows that he brings an added quality to the side every minute he is on the pitch. And yet despite this we went to Elland Road and, until losing yet another international midfielder (Nicky Butt) to injury, totally dominated the game.

If we have a problem at the moment it's that we are failing to find the net with the regularity we normally do. It's something that won't last.

By the time Leeds nicked their goal we could have been four up, but football doesn't work that way, and so we have to wait for the time when the luck swings back our way. And when it does, be sure that you're not one of the so called 'fans' who've spouted off and against our beloved shirts to a thirsty football public just 'loving it' that we're not dominating the domestic game that we've taken to new levels over the past decade. **SB**

> "We lacked a bit of luck at times, but we played some fantastic football. We outplayed them for 45 minutes"
>
> SIR ALEX FERGUSON

What the papers said...

'Leeds United beat Manchester United for the first time in 11 attempts to bring about a second defeat in four days for Sir Alex Ferguson's struggling side, who started the season as title favourites but have just recorded their worst start to the Premiership. Problems are beginning to build up at Old Trafford.'
Paul Wilson, The Observer

'Beckham's flailing arm deflected the focus away from Ferdinand, who was given a predictably fierce welcome following his summer switch across the Pennines. The England defender was jeered by a small mob of angry fans as United's heavily guarded team bus pulled into a back entrance of Elland Road. Taunts of "Scum" were hurled his way and when he took the pitch chants of "Judas" and "One greedy b******" rained form the stands.'
Paul McCarthy, The People

Manchester United
GIGGS (9 MINS), SOLSKJAER (35 MINS), VERON (46 MINS), VAN NISTELROOY (54 MINS), FORLAN (PEN 89)

5

Maccabi Haifa
KATAN (6 MINS), COHEN (85 MINS)

2

WED 18 SEPTEMBER 02 ◆ 7.45PM ◆ OLD TRAFFORD ◆ ATT: 63, 439 ◆ CL PHASE ONE ◆ REF: P ALLEARTS ◆ ENTERTAINMENT: ✪✪✪✪✪

Wahey! Diego Forlan scores his first goal for United

THE TEAMS

BARTHEZ 6
FERDINAND 6   BLANC 6
O'SHEA 6   SILVESTRE 6
VERON 8   P NEVILLE 8
BECKHAM 7   GIGGS 7
VAN NISTELROOY 7   SOLSKJAER 6

LANDBERG   KATAN   ROSSO
PRALIJA   ALMOSHNINO   BADIR
KEISE   EJIOFOR   BENADO   HARAZI
AWAT

United Subs Forlan 7 for Giggs (56), Ricardo 6 for Barthez (67), Pugh 6 for Van Nistelrooy (75)
Maccabi Subs Zano for Almoshnino (56), Israllevich for Zandberg (64), Cohen for Harazi (73)

MATCH STATS

MANCHESTER UNITED		MACCABI HAIFA
60%	POSSESSION	40%
15	SHOTS ON TARGET	5
7	SHOTS OFF TARGET	5
12	CORNERS	2
7	FOULS CONCEDED	11
0	BOOKINGS	1
0	RED CARDS	0

United star man ★
Seba Veron Confident and assured

Welcome win boosts the spirits

> "I think I'd have been hated by 67,000 people if I had denied Diego the penalty!"
>
> DAVID BECKHAM

FOLLOWING TWO DEFEATS AND GENUINE CONCERN THAT ALL WAS NOT WELL AT OLD TRAFFORD, UNITED WERE UNDER PRESSURE TO WIN EASILY AGAINST THE ISRAELI CHAMPIONS...

THE GAME KICKED OFF UNITED'S eighth Champions League campaign, a record matched but not bettered by any other team.

Sir Alex had complimented the wrong Israeli team before the match but he was well intentioned when he spoke of advancements in the standard of Israeli football. Haifa proved as much in becoming the first Israeli team to qualify for UEFA's gravy train, and backed by over 4,000 fans – the largest ever visiting contingent at Old Trafford in the Champions League – they were intent on enjoying the experience.

The fans, a mass of green who clapped, jumped and swayed to their own rhythm, seemed content just to be watching their team at Old Trafford and they celebrated disbelievingly when Katan gave Haifa the lead after eight minutes.

Giggs, who has incurred recent criticism from United fans unhappy with his form, equalised a minute later, heading home from a Phil Neville cross. And he continued to cause problems. United applied further pressure and had it not been for the heroics of keeper Awate, would have taken a 2–1 lead well before Solskjaer did eventually make it two on 35 minutes.

Veron, who also has critics among matchgoing Reds, struck a third a minute after half-time as the self belief and confidence began to rise.

"Are you watching Liverpool?" sang Reds gleefully, a reference to Liverpool's 2–0 European defeat to Valencia the night before.

When Van Nistelrooy made it 4–1 after 54 minutes, Sir Alex began a series of substitutions, ensuring that the new Castillian goalkeeper Ricardo and Danny Pugh were introduced for their competitive debuts. But the loudest cheer came when Diego Forlan came on. Over 14 hours in a red shirt without a goal but the fans have continued to support him.

With 35 minutes to score, it looked like he was in for more frustration but in the 89th minute, United were awarded a penalty. "Diego, Diego" roared the crowd, and captain Beckham bowed to the pressure to let the Uruguayan score his first goal.

It might have been a penalty, but it was a goal no less. It was a moment and a night to enjoy, but tougher tests lie ahead. **SB**

THE TEAMS

BARTHEZ ⑥

P NEVILLE ⑦ FERDINAND ⑦ O'SHEA ⑦ SILVESTRE ⑦

BECKHAM ⑦ BUTT ⑦ VERON ⑦ GIGGS ⑦

VAN NISTELROOY ⑦ ☐ SOLSKJAER ⑥

SHERINGHAM KEANE

ETHERINGTON BUNJEVCEVIC REDKNAPP IVERSEN

THATCHER DOHERTY RICHARDS ☐ DAVIES

KELLER

United Subs G Neville ⑥ for Veron (76), Forlan ⑥ for Solskjaer (76), Pugh ⑥ for Giggs (85) **Spurs Subs** Les Ferdinand for Iversen (76), Acimovic for Sheringham (85)

MATCH STATS

MANCHESTER UNITED		TOTTENHAM HOTSPUR
50%	POSSESSION	50%
8	SHOTS ON TARGET	3
8	SHOTS OFF TARGET	5
10	CORNERS	5
13	FOULS CONCEDED	9
1	BOOKINGS	1
0	RED CARDS	0

United star man ★

Fabien Barthez United's 'number one' on the day

Manchester United
VAN NISTELROOY (63 MINS)

Tottenham Hotspur

1
0

SAT 21 SEPTEMBER 02 ◆ 3PM ◆ OLD TRAFFORD ◆ ATT: 67,611 ◆ FA PREMIERSHIP ◆ REF: R STYLES ◆ ENTERTAINMENT: ●●●○○

Ruud beats Kasey Keller (at last!) from the penalty spot

One-nil (again) to the United

THE LAST THING YOU NEED WHEN YOU'RE STRUGGLING TO SCORE GOALS IS TO COME UP AGAINST A GOALKEEPER IN INSPIRED FORM.

UNFORTUNATELY FOR US, SPURS 'keeper Kasey Keller was so outstanding in this game that the Man of the Match award could have been presented to him at half-time.

Our games with Tottenham Hotspur have tended to be pretty outstanding of late too. Last season we shared 12 goals with them in the two fixtures, and the football served up by both teams was sublime. This year, with both teams ravaged by injuries, the same wasn't expected. But we were wrong to let such negative thoughts enter our minds, as both sides stuck true to their traditions and served us

up a really entertaining game.

As the match went on and the deadlock remained unbroken, however, thoughts started to slip back to the games against Leeds, Bolton, Sunderland and Chelsea – all matches in which failing to score at times in the game when we were creating freely and dominating cost us. But while the effort level remains elevated despite crucial missing personnel, there is still enough guile and style to worry all teams. Tottenham, falsely sitting near the the top of the Premiership when the game kicked off, were no different.

When Ruud 'tumbled' at the hands and feet of Gary Doherty, the referee saw it as the result of a fair challenge. But the felling of Ole Gunnar by the same culprit just a minute later resulted in the penalty from which we'd just been robbed. Even if Solskjaer had merely been breathed upon, the penalty would probably

> **"It doesn't matter what form they are in, Manchester United always ask you questions"**
>
> GLENN HODDLE

have been given such was the magnitude of the initial mistake. But as it happened, Ole was cut down almost as harshly, and Ruud took the opportunity to beat Keller for the only time in the game.

With seconds left, and with the game still in the balance, Barthez for the second time in the game was called upon to make a world-class stop. Those who have recently questioned just who our 'number one' really is, had their question answered. Fabien saved, United had three points.

In fairness, it was the performances of both 'keepers that ensured the game didn't end up with the sort of surreal 5–3 scoreline we'd witnessed at White Hart Lane a year ago. But credit must go to both teams. If the players injured or unavailable through suspension could have been pooled you'd probably have had a pretty good line-up. But those available on the day made sure of a decent spectacle. **SB**

Bayer Leverkusen BERBATOV (52 MINS) | 1

Manchester United VAN NISTELROOY (31, 44 MINS) | 2

TUE 24 SEPTEMBER 02 ◆ 7.45GMT ◆ BAYARENA ◆ ATT: 22,500 ◆ CL PHASE ONE ◆ REF: J.WEGEREEF ◆ ENTERTAINMENT: ✪✪✪✪✪

'Van Miss-elrooy, er, doesn't miss. 2–0'

THE TEAMS

JURIC
ZIVKOVIC — RAMELOW — LUCIO
BALITSCH — BABIC
NEUVILLE — SCHNEIDER — OJIGWE
BASTURK — BRDARIC

VAN NISTELROOY ⑧
VERON ⑦ — GIGGS ⑥ — BECKHAM ⑦
BUTT ⑦ — P NEVILLE ⑥
SILVESTRE ⑥ — O'SHEA ⑦
BLANC ⑦ — FERDINAND ⑦
BARTHEZ ⑦

Bayer Subs Berbatov for Neuville (22), Simak for Ojigwe (64), Franca for Balitsch (81)
United Subs Forlan ⑥ for Van Nistelrooy (45), G Neville ⑥ for O'Shea (45), Solskjaer ⑤ for Veron (88)

MATCH STATS

BAYER LEVERKUSEN		MANCHESTER UNITED
53%	POSSESSION	47%
3	SHOTS ON TARGET	2
9	SHOTS OFF TARGET	3
7	CORNERS	0
9	FOULS CONCEDED	18
1	BOOKINGS	3
0	RED CARDS	0

United star man ⭐

Ruud van Nistelrooy Silenced his critics

Defence holds on for revenge win...

> "Ruud hasn't lost any of his confidence. He will score plenty of goals this season"
>
> OLE GUNNAR SOLSKJAER

WHEN THE DRAW FOR GROUP F WAS MADE, MOST PEOPLE PREDICTED THAT THE TOP TWO PLACES WOULD GO ON TO BE OCCUPIED BY UNITED AND THE TEAM WHO ENDED OUR DREAMS OF HAMPDEN LAST SEASON, BAYER LEVERKUSEN.

SO FAR ONLY ONE OF THE TWO TEAMS is living up to their pre-group billing and, fortunately, it's us.

As the cliché goes, 'it was a game of two halves'. The first 45 minutes saw United play neat counterattacking football and take a two-goal lead. The second saw them concede an early goal then put on a stalwart defensive display to hang on to what they'd got. Yes, you read it here – a stalwart

defensive display. A sign, hopefully, that last season's problems at the back are in the process of being eradicated.

"Rio, Rio, he is a Red you know…" sang the travelling fans, showing who they believe is responsible for the tighter defensive displays, but all the defenders deserve credit for this display because it was backs to the walls for most of the second half. But unlike at times last season, the team didn't cave in when the opposition put them under intense pressure.

The five-man midfield has been the focus of plenty of criticism from some but in this game it worked a treat. Veron was able to make a telling contribution with his passing, Beckham played a captain's role slightly further right and Nicky Butt showed once again why he's become a regular in the middle of Sven Goran Eriksson's England midfield. Add to that Giggsy causing problems

and an excellent Phil Neville breaking up Bayer attacks and you've the answer to the question 'why play 5–4–1?' Away from home against tough opposition it suits us better.

It's been 30 years since we won in Germany but this one was worth waiting for. Making a mockery of his 'crisis' in confidence Ruud van Nistelrooy scored twice. Sadly that is all he managed before a hamstring injury cut short his return to goal-getting form. However, we'd seen enough to know that headlines like 'Ruud van Miss-elrooy' were as wide of the mark as the media had claimed his shooting was.

Football has a habit of producing unexpected twists and turns and, while no-one wants to be accused of speaking too soon, surely now, having collected six of Sir Alex's ten point target for the first group phase, the Reds have made things easier for themselves. For once. **PD**

THE TEAMS

KIELY

YOUNG   RUFUS   FORTUNE   POWELL

ROBINSON   MUSTOE   JENSEN   KONCHESKY

BARTLETT

EUELL

SOLSKJAER 6

GIGGS 8   SCHOLES 8   FORLAN 6

BUTT 6   BECKHAM 7

P NEVILLE 6   O'SHEA 7

BLANC 6   FERDINAND 7

BARTHEZ 6

Charlton Subs Johansson for Young (85), Kishishev for Mustoe (88) **United Subs** Van Nistelrooy 8 for Forlan (58), G Neville 7 for Butt (70)

MATCH STATS

CHARLTON ATHLETIC		MANCHESTER UNITED
44%	POSSESSION	56%
2	SHOTS ON TARGET	6
4	SHOTS OFF TARGET	6
3	CORNERS	6
14	FOULS CONCEDED	10
3	BOOKINGS	4
0	RED CARDS	0

United star man ★

Ryan Giggs Charlton had no answer to his movement

Charlton Athletic JENSEN (43) 1
Manchester United SCHOLES (54), GIGGS (83), VAN NISTELROOY (90) 3

SAT 28 SEPTEMBER 02 ◆ 3PM ◆ THE VALLEY ◆ ATT: 26,630 ◆ FA PREMIERSHIP ◆ REF: D GALLAGHER ◆ ENTERTAINMENT: ✪✪✪✪○

Genius at work

Reds rewarded for resilience and fluidity

"THE RESILIENCE OF MY TEAM IS THERE FOR ALL TO SEE. THEY NEVER GIVE IN AND WHEN YOU HAVE THESE QUALITIES YOU'VE ALWAYS GOT A CHANCE." SIR ALEX FERGUSON'S POST-MATCH REMARK SAID IT ALL.

THE VALLEY HASN'T BEEN A HAPPY hunting ground for Manchester United in recent seasons and when Paul Scholes' excellent shot was cleared off the line and Claus Jensen put the Addicks in front on the stroke of half-time it was hard not to start getting a bit edgy. With Arsenal having already ripped Leeds United to shreds earlier in the day, we simply couldn't afford to lose. The players knew that as well as anyone and they

weren't about to give up the three points without a fight.

Neither was Alex Ferguson, who ordered Ruud van Nistelrooy (on the bench protecting a tight hamstring) to warm up as soon as the second half kicked off. As it happened, those already on the pitch managed to conjure the equaliser without the Dutchman – Paul Scholes guiding home a Ryan Giggs cross. But the importance of Ruud's introduction a minute later can't be underestimated. His strength in holding up the ball and bringing others in to play is second to none and Charlton just couldn't cope with him. His running and movement were also the perfect foil for Scholes and Giggs.

"We might think they play 4–4–2 or whatever but where do players like Giggs actually play?" asked bemused Charlton manager Alan Curbishley afterwards. "They move, keep the ball and move some more. The great

"I could have set Ruud up earlier when I pulled one back but the keeper saved it. Ruud was giving me dirty looks after that so I thought I'd better set him up at the end!"

RYAN GIGGS

sides have that fluidity. Just look at Brazil in the World Cup finals last summer. What was their formation?"

Giggs highlighted Curbishley's point in the closing stages of the game. The 'left-winger' cut through the middle and dribbled round Dean Kiely for United's second on 83 minutes before popping up on the right wing and delivering an inch-perfect cross – with his right foot – onto Ruud's head for the third in injury time.

It was no less than Manchester United deserved, but the players had had to work their socks off to get it. "This wasn't an easy game for them and they really had to earn their victory," was the accurate assessment of Addicks' left back Chris Powell after the game.

Grinding out a hard-fought win? Isn't that a classic symptom of championship-winning form? Only time will tell, but it makes great viewing in the meantime. **SS**

CHAPTER TWO

EURO FUN
DOMESTIC STRESS

THE UNITED TEAM STEAMING through the first phase of the Champions League was almost unrecognisable from the side struggling in the league. With Seba Veron pulling the strings in midfield and Ruud Van Nistelrooy firing in the goals, United looked dominant in Europe. But in the absence of the injured Roy Keane, United's league performances lacked purpose and consistency. Points were being dropped far too easily and, after an appalling derby display, Red hopes of regaining the title were already fading.

Tuesday 1 October
OLYMPIAKOS (H)
CHAMPIONS LEAGUE PHASE ONE

Monday 7 October
EVERTON (H)
PREMIERSHIP

Saturday 19 October
FULHAM (A)
PREMIERSHIP

Wednesday 23 October
OLYMPIAKOS (A)
CHAMPIONS LEAGUE PHASE ONE

Saturday 26 October
ASTON VILLA (H)
PREMIERSHIP

Tuesday 29 October
MACCABI HAIFA (A)
CHAMPIONS LEAGUE PHASE ONE

Saturday 2 November
SOUTHAMPTON (H)
PREMIERSHIP

Wednesday 6 November
LEICESTER CITY (H)
WORTHINGTON CUP RD 3

Saturday 9 November
MANCHESTER CITY (A)
PREMIERSHIP

Manchester United
GIGGS 2 (19, 66), VERON (26), SOLSKJAER (77)

Olympiakos

4

0

TUE 1 OCT 02 ◆ 7.45PM ◆ OLD TRAFFORD ◆ ATT: 66,902 ◆ CL PHASE ONE ◆ REF: GILLES VEISSIERE ◆ ENTERTAINMENT: ✪✪✪✪

"That goal was good enough to eat, Seba"

THE TEAMS

BARTHEZ ⑥

FERDINAND ⑥   BLANC ⑥

G NEVILLE ⑥   SILVESTRE ⑦

BUTT ⑦   VERON ⑧

BECKHAM ⑦   GIGGS ⑦

SOLSKJAER ⑦   SCHOLES ⑦

OFORI QUAYE

DJORDJEVIC   ZETTERBERG   GIANNAKOPOULOS

ZE ELIAS ■   KAREMBEU

VENETIDIS

ANTZAS   ANATOLAKIS   AMANATIDIS

ELEFTHEROPOULOS

United Subs Fortune ⑥ for Giggs (69), O'Shea ⑥ for Blanc (69), Forlan ⑥ for Scholes (77),
Olympiakos Subs Dracena for Giannakopoulos (45), Alexandris for Ofori Quaye (59), Patsatzoglou for Amanatidis (73),

MATCH STATS

MANCHESTER UNITED		OLYMPIAKOS
62%	POSSESSION	38%
9	SHOTS ON TARGET	2
3	SHOTS OFF TARGET	4
4	CORNERS	0
16	FOULS CONCEDED	14
3	BOOKINGS	2
0	RED CARDS	1

United star man ★

Seba Veron In total control

Greeks brushed aside by visionary Veron

> "Seba's goal was world class. You will struggle to see a better goal in Europe this week. It was a fantastic bit of football in the build-up and then he had the audacity to chip the goalkeeper"
>
> SIR ALEX FERGUSON

IF YOU DIDN'T KNOW BETTER YOU'D THINK THERE WERE TWO SEPARATE TEAMS PLAYING AT OLD TRAFFORD THIS SEASON.

THE FREE-FLOWING XI THAT PLAY IN the Champions League and the goal-shy unit that have been turning out in the Premiership.

Three Champions League matches at OT have now returned 14 goals, an amazing tally from a team who managed only three in their first four games domestically. It's a strange situation, but surely only a matter of time before home performances like this one extend to the league.

Anybody who is anybody has an opinion about United's current plight. Yes, we lack cover up front, we miss Roy Keane and a few have

not been in great form since August, but to suggest a great team can become a mediocre one overnight is ridiculous. From the outset of this game the players, even without the injured Ruud, gave their response.

While most of us were trying to adjust to seeing United in blue, they set about Olympiakos with a speed and vigour that soon made us forget about the colour of their shirts. Chances for Beckham, Scholes and even Gary Neville were followed by the opening goal from Ryan Giggs, who seems to have rediscovered the knack of scoring at home.

Undoubtedly, though, the half, if not the match, belonged to Seba Veron. He dominated the midfield, dictated the play, sliced the Greek defence open with some visionary passes and crowned his display with a goal that simply oozed class. His cheeky chip over Eleftheropoulos brought the house down and even his

staunchest critic couldn't deny him the standing ovation he received at both half and full-time.

The second half was a calmer affair. Olympiakos, who had Ze Elias sent off just before the break for a wild challenge on Veron, were content with damage limitation and the crowd were recovering from an impromptu half-time marriage proposal.

A bizarre third goal, when Giggs' cross was deflected home by Greek defender Anatolakis, and a cool Solskjaer finish from his only real chance of the game rounded off the scoring and put United six points clear at the top of Group F.

One point from our remaining three games will see us comfortably through to the second group stage. While continued performances with this level of assuredness will see us progress still further in the competition. Old Trafford on 28 May? You've got to have a dream! **RS**

THE TEAMS

BARTHEZ 7

O'SHEA 8   BLANC 8

G NEVILLE 8   SILVESTRE 7

SCHOLES 8   BUTT 7

BECKHAM 7   VERON 6

VAN NISTELROOY 6   GIGGS 6

RADZINSKI   CAMPBELL

PEMBRIDGE   CARSLEY

GRAVESON   LI TIE

UNSWORTH   WEIR   YOBO   HIBBERT

WRIGHT

United Subs Solskjaer 7 for Veron (63), Forlan 6 for Butt (85), P Neville 7 for Van Nistelrooy (89), **Everton Subs** Rooney for Radzinski (74)

MATCH STATS

MANCHESTER UNITED		EVERTON
58%	POSSESSION	42%
5	SHOTS ON TARGET	2
7	SHOTS OFF TARGET	5
7	CORNERS	1
15	FOULS CONCEDED	14
0	BOOKINGS	2
0	RED CARDS	0

United star man

John O'Shea Youngster looked the part next to Blanc

Manchester United 3
SCHOLES 2 (86, 90), VAN NISTELROOY (90)
Everton 0

MON 7 OCTOBER 02 ◆ 8PM ◆ OLD TRAFFORD ◆ ATT: 67,629 ◆ FA PREMIERSHIP ◆ REF: M.RILEY ◆ ENTERTAINMENT: ✪✪✪✪✪

Two-goal Scholesy celebrates

A bad night to leave early

AND THEN THERE WERE THREE. AS WE WAITED FOR – AND WILLED – A LATE UNITED WINNER, HOPES FOR A WEST BROM-TYPE FINALE WERE BALANCED WITH THE FEAR THAT WE COULD SUCCUMB TO A BOLTON-LIKE SUCKER PUNCH.

As the game drew to its conclusion, it really opened up and the impressive Everton substitute that is the young tank Wayne Rooney nearly charged his way through in the 84th minute only for Fabien Barthez to block his effort.

United fans could breathe out again with relief and then use their lungs to urge one final, last charge.

Yet we should know this team better by now. Why have one closing attack when several will do – like the proverbial buses we waited ages for one goal, only to see three turn up at once. It was a heartening sign.

Up until then I would find it hard to join the calls that this was a great game. It was undoubtedly exciting at times and some of our passing play had been excellent. We were switching sides quickly, holding possession at length and making some sweeping moves forward. Yet there did seem a lack of invention and a penchant to want to walk the ball into the Everton net. Yet as we've seen all season, we kept creating chances and the grand finale merely highlighted what can happen when we start taking them. Scholes' spectacular goal on the stroke of full time was not just the strike of the match but a real boost to his, and our, confidence.

John O'Shea also continued to

> "That was one of the best games I've seen for many a day and it's the best Everton team I've seen for years. We really had to perform well to win. The score doesn't tell the story of the match"
> SIR ALEX FERGUSON

augment his early season reputation with an outstanding display. Becks may have won the Man of the Match award on TV for his tireless effort and running but the young defender must have chased him close. He lapped up everything that came his way, cajoled through every move by his wily old colleague Laurent Blanc. What benefit Blanc's presence must make to the learning curve of our youngsters. Laurent the coach maybe?

The *Manchester Evening News* had earlier reported Fergie's appreciation for evening matches at Old Trafford and their improved atmospheres. If it were a call to arms it worked a treat as the Singing End coaxed the whole of Old Trafford into a cracking crescendo, personified by a first half period of intense noise. It was like the good old days. And on a Monday night, too. Naturally, it just had you wondering why it can't be like that for every game. **BC**

Fulham MARLET (15) | 1
Manchester United SOLSKJAER (62) | 1

SAT 19 OCT 02 ◆ 3PM ◆ LOFTUS ROAD ◆ ATT: 18,103 ◆ FA PREMIERSHIP ◆ REF: M DEAN ◆ ENTERTAINMENT: ✪✪✪✪✪

Becks plans his next move

THE TEAMS

	VAN DER SAR		
	KNIGHT	GOMA	
OUADDOU			BREVETT
	LEGWINSKI	DAVIS	
FINNAN			MALBRANQUE
	SAVA	MARLET	

GIGGS ⑥	SOLSKJAER ⑦	BECKHAM ⑦
	SCHOLES ⑦	
	P NEVILLE ⑥ VERON ⑥	
SILVESTRE ⑥		G NEVILLE ⑦
	O'SHEA ⑦ BLANC ⑦	
	BARTHEZ ⑧	

United Subs Fortune ⑥ for P Neville (59), Forlan ⑥ for Silvestre (81),
Fulham Subs Hayles for Sava (79)

MATCH STATS

FULHAM		MANCHESTER UNITED
47%	POSSESSION	53%
7	SHOTS ON TARGET	6
7	SHOTS OFF TARGET	3
6	CORNERS	1
10	FOULS CONCEDED	15
1	BOOKINGS	3
0	RED CARDS	0

United star man ★

Fabien Barthez Crucial saves throughout

One point gained after busy week

> "Fabien is a professional and professionals do those kind of things. Players have been doing that for years, but I've got no complaints about the yellow card"
>
> SIR ALEX FERGUSON

LEAVING THE GROUND WE HEARD THAT ARSENAL'S IMPRESSIVE RUN HAD ENDED. AT FIRST EVERYONE GROANED, FOR THIS SEEMED LIKE TWO POINTS DROPPED AND A CHANCE MISSED TO BEGIN TO CLOSE THE POINTS GAP.

BUT SOON THE REALISATION DAWNED that Arsene Wenger's talk of an unbeaten season had ended as early as October and despite our stuttering start to the campaign, we're clearly still in touch.

With Ruud and Nicky Butt the latest casualties, Fulham got into their stride quicker than United, benefiting from the recent break in Premiership action. But there lies the rub. For while Fulham's players have had the chance to re-charge their early season batteries, United's have been traipsing off playing a heavy international fixture list – and it showed. We may have matched Fulham for the first hour, but at no time did we really get to grips with a game which saw Fabien make several crucial saves to keep us in the game. Certainly nobody could complain about the half-time scoreline.

But when Ole pounced on a bit of a mix-up in the Fulham defence and hammered home the equaliser, the whole complexion of the game changed. Where Fulham had marked tightly, pushing Finnan forward on Silvestre and giving our players no time on the ball, it was now United in the ascendancy, and it seemed only a matter of time before a second.

Unfortunately, the referee and his assistants then had a crucial bearing on events, firstly awarding a penalty to Fulham after Blanc's innocuous challenge on Marlet, then failing to spot a clear hand-ball in the Fulham penalty area. Justice was done, though, with Barthez once again coming to the rescue. Some might charge him with 'unsporting' behaviour in making Malbranque wait to take the kick, but he's certainly entitled to clear his boots – and his thoughts – for the task in hand. Anyway, at the time the referee was occupied with a bit of shoving that was going on while the kick was waiting to be taken.

In the cold light of the following morning, the two points dropped began to seem more of a point gained. What will be worrying Fergie, however, is the continued absence of Ruud and therefore goals. With Keano still out for a while, and niggling injuries to our England quintet, it could be a farly long slog to Christmas. **SB**

THE TEAMS

ELEFTHEROPOULOS

ANATOLAKIS ☐   ANTZAS

PATSATZOGLOU   VENETIDIS

KAREMBEU

ZETTERBERG   DRACENA

GIANNAKOPOULOS   DJORDJEVIC

GIOVANNI

FORLAN ❼

GIGGS ❼   BECKHAM ❻

VERON ❽   SCHOLES ❾

P NEVILLE ❼

SILVESTRE ❻   G NEVILLE ❼ ☐

BLANC ❼   O'SHEA ❻

BARTHEZ ❼

Olympiakos Subs Choutos for Giovanni (45), Ofori Quaye for Zetterberg (71), Mavrogenidis for Giannakopoulos (88)
United Subs Chadwick ❺ for Beckham (63), Fortune ❺ for Giggs (63), Richardson ❼ for Veron (87)

MATCH STATS

OLYMPIAKOS		MANCHESTER UNITED
43%	POSSESSION	57%
3	SHOTS ON TARGET	6
9	SHOTS OFF TARGET	6
0	CORNERS	8
15	FOULS CONCEDED	14
2	BOOKINGS	1
0	RED CARDS	0

United star man ★

Paul Scholes His long-range shooting paid dividends

Olympiakos CHOUTOS (70), DJORDJEVIC (76)

Manchester United BLANC (21), VERON (59), SCHOLES (84)

2
3

WED 23 OCT 02 ◆ 7.45GMT ◆ APOLLON RIZOUPOLIS ST. ◆ ATT: 15,000 ◆ CL PHASE ONE ◆ REF: P COLLINA ◆ ENTERTAINMENT ✪✪✪✪

Becks congratulates Seba on his fine goal

Reds leave Greek champions feeling blue

THIS WAS OUR HUNDREDTH WIN IN EUROPE, AND IF ON THE HOUR YOU'D ASKED ANYBODY STOOD IN THE BALMY WARMTH OF AN ATHENS EVENING THEY'D PROBABLY HAVE RATED IT AS ONE OF OUR EASIER EUROPEAN VICTORIES.

WITH SCHOLES IN IMPERIOUS FORM, the score at half-time might have shown a slender one-goal lead, but the gulf between the sides was huge. Even the vociferous Greek following, which we'd expected to give us a similarly heated welcome to the one we received last year, were muted from the moment Pierluigi Collina blew his whistle to get the game underway. So when Seba added a superb second just before the hour mark, everybody in the stadium knew it was game over.

With nine points won even before this fixture, and with the game now 'dead' as a contest, Fergie was thus allowed the luxury of removing the battle-scarred Beckham and Giggs.

Both players have not only been performing for club, but also tirelessly for their countries in some very big European Championship qualifiers, and would no doubt have been grateful for an early night.

However as often happens when changes are made, within seconds Olympiakos pulled a goal back through substitute Lampros Choutos and suddenly the tiny stadium of the Greek champions came alive.

For the first time in the match, Olympiakos now enjoyed a bit of possession. With only three sides of the ground open to spectators (one end just had hoardings), you'd be forgiven for thinking the atmosphere

> "We knew it was going to take something special to get us back in front and that's what Paul came up with"
>
> PHIL NEVILLE

would be sterile. But as the Greeks pressed forward, it was the noise from behind that drove them on. Predrag Djordjevic, who had seemed out of sorts all night but had looked a more than decent player only a couple of weeks ago at Old Trafford, charged forward. As our defence stood off him, he unleashed a low drive to level the scores. Red heads that moments earlier had been nodding in admiration now shook in disbelief.

We needn't have worried, though. While the other 10 players had started making heavy weather of the contest, Scholesy (whose intentions had been clear from his speculative 45-yard shot early on) took the responsibility upon himself to ensure the right result. After one long-range effort hit the post, his second in as many minutes made the most of some ordinary goalkeeping and kept up our 100 per cent record. Qualification for phase two is now assured, with two games still to go. **SB**

Manchester United FORLAN (79) **1**
Aston Villa MELLBERG (35) **1**

SAT 26 OCT 02 ◆ 3PM ◆ OLD TRAFFORD ◆ ATT:67,619 ◆ FA PREMIERSHIP ◆ REF: GRAHAM POLL ◆ ENTERTAINMENT: ●●●●●

THE TEAMS

BARTHEZ Ⓖ
FERDINAND Ⓖ　BLANC Ⓢ
G NEVILLE Ⓖ　　　P NEVILLE Ⓖ　　SILVESTRE Ⓢ
VERON Ⓖ
BECKHAM Ⓖ　　　　　　　　　　　SOLSKJAER Ⓢ
SCHOLES Ⓖ　FORLAN Ⓖ

DUBLIN
MOORE
SAMUEL　　　　　　　　　　　　　LEONHARDSON
TAYLOR　KINSELLA
BARRY　　　　　　　　　　　　　DELANEY
MELLBERG　STAUNTON
ENCKELMAN

United Subs Fortune Ⓖ for P Neville (60)
Villa Subs Angel for Moore (66), Crouch for Dublin (66), Hitzlsperger for Leonhardsen (84)

MATCH STATS

MANCHESTER UNITED		ASTON VILLA
44%	POSSESSION	56%
2	SHOTS ON TARGET	6
4	SHOTS OFF TARGET	6
3	CORNERS	6
14	FOULS CONCEDED	10
2	BOOKINGS	3
0	RED CARDS	0

United star man ★

Paul Scholes A constant menace

Our favourite Uruguayan shows off his six-pack after nicking an equaliser

Diego scores in open play!

> "There's a difference managing a team of this size because the expectations are huge. Everyone wants to beat them. You won't find me criticising United's season"
>
> GRAHAM TAYLOR

THE EUROPEAN CUP, SEVEN LEAGUE CHAMPIONSHIPS, FOUR FA CUPS, THREE DOUBLES, A TREBLE, THE WORLD CLUB CHAMPIONSHIP – SO WHERE DID IT ALL GO WRONG?

SOME MAY THINK IT CHURLISH TO SAY but on a drab Manchester day, most United supporters would rather have been almost anywhere else except at Old Trafford watching this painful performance.

With only 12 goals in the last 11 home league games, it's not too difficult to pinpoint the team's problems. And it's not as if behind that statistic lies an unlucky story of missed chances and wondrous opposition goalkeeping. The fact is Manchester United weren't attacking with the pace, verve and invention we expect from our heroes and, after 10 months' worth of struggle against supposedly inferior opposition teams on home soil, the question many supporters will be wondering is whether the current team can turn this situation around. OK, so United were suffering a few injuries after their trip to Athens, but wasn't the team in Red good enough to win?

No-one's demanding miracles: sure, teams have off-days and all credit to Aston Villa, their spirited performance belied their own early season woes, but is it too much to expect United to take the game to the opposition?

Until Mellberg's goal there was barely a single United player who appeared able to wrest control from the opposition. Hardly what's expected of a team such as Manchester United, which is packed with international-class footballers.

While United did eventually hit back to equalise through Diego Forlan (even the PA operator couldn't believe it – instead attributing the goal to David Beckham), Liverpool's win over Tottenham meant this was yet another two points dropped at home. The fact that we are reliant on such unproven youngsters like Forlan despite the team having had over £100m invested in it over the past couple of seasons is also a worrying sign.

But give the Uruguayan his place in the sun – everyone in the ground was delighted to see him break his Premiership duck, and he's definitely a player who should turn out to be a success in the long-term. Whatever the future holds, be it success or failure, the only demand we place is that we do it in style, the United way.

Not like today. **JPO**

THE TEAMS

AWAT

ZANO   HARAZI   BENADO   KEISE

BADIR   ZAUTATIS   PRALIJA

ROSSO   KATAN

AYEGBINI

FORLAN **5**
RICHARDSON **6**   SCHOLES **7**   SOLSKJAER **5**
FORTUNE **5**   P NEVILLE **6**
SILVESTRE **6**   G NEVILLE **5**
O'SHEA **6**   FERDINAND **6**
RICARDO **5**

Haifa Subs Zandberg for Zautatis (82), Almoshnino for Ayegbini (84) **United Subs** Nardiello **6** for Richardson (59), Timm **5** for Forlan (80)

MATCH STATS

HAIFA		MANCHESTER UNITED
40%	POSSESSION	60%
5	SHOTS ON TARGET	4
5	SHOTS OFF TARGET	13
1	CORNERS	11
16	FOULS CONCEDED	12
0	BOOKINGS	3
0	RED CARDS	0

United star man ★

Paul Scholes Did his best to support the youngsters

Maccabi Haifa
KATAN (40), ZAUTATAS (56), AYEGBINI (PEN 77)
Manchester United

3

0

TUE 29 OCT 02 ◆ 7.45PM GMT ◆ GSP STADIUM, NICOSIA ◆ ATT: 22,000 ◆ CL PHASE ONE ◆ REF: LOPEZ NIETO ◆ ENTERTAINMENT ●●○○○

Zautatas' incredible strike flies in the top corner

New boys add meaning to dull affair

GRANTED, IT WAS A WEAKENED SIDE THAT SIR ALEX SENT OUT FOR THIS MATCH AGAINST THE ISRAELI CHAMPIONS, BUT IT SHOULD STILL HAVE BEEN STRONG ENOUGH TO WIN.

WITH GIGGS, BECKHAM, VERON, Barthez and Blanc all resting at home and the injury list still including Keane, Van Nistelrooy, Butt and Brown, it was always going to be tough for the youngsters coming in. Kieran Richardson was given his first start, as was reserve keeper Ricardo, and the bench contained young guns Mads Timm, Daniel Nardiello, Danny Pugh, Lee Roche and Mark Lynch. The manager was clearly using the match as an opportunity to give valuable experience to his youngsters.

Before the game, few in the stadium – apart from possibly a few disappointed Cypriot Reds and British holidaymakers – could argue with the manager's decision to leave so many of his stars at home. There are some big matches ahead and this game was almost irrelevant, due to us having already secured qualification from the group.

There was some disappointment that the team wasn't stronger but we still had a total of 10 internationals in the starting 11 and should have seen off Haifa. We didn't.

Despite making a good start, we failed to make our possession count with goals and by the time Maccabi took the lead through an unstoppable shot, we should have been in front. Instead, Katan's wonder goal just seemed to knock the stuffing out of us.

Throughout the game, the 10,000

> "There was nothing for us to lose in playing some youngsters. They can always learn something"
>
> SIR ALEX FERGUSON

or so Maccabi fans created a fantastic atmosphere. They bounced, chanted and roared their team on constantly in the first half and as the second began seemed to increase the volume again. They were clearly anticipating more goals and were rewarded early in the second half when Zautatas produced a strike that may even have surpassed his side's first wonder goal.

When Ricardo conceded a penalty for the third, the Haifa fans wildly celebrated their club's greatest ever victory. Given their vociferous support, they deserved their moment of happiness.

In the away end on the other hand, the moans and groans from some Reds started long before the final whistle sounded. Hopefully though, we will all see the benefits of the manager's decision to leave our stars at home in the form of good results in coming weeks. **PD**

Manchester United P NEVILLE (15), FORLAN (85)

2

Southampton FERNANDES (35)

1

SAT 2 NOV 02 ◆ 3PM ◆ OLD TRAFFORD ◆ ATT: 67,691 ◆ FA PREMIERSHIP ◆ REF: U.RENNIE ◆ ENTERTAINMENT: ●●●●○

D–I–E–G–O! The shirt's off again...

THE TEAMS

BARTHEZ ❽

FERDINAND ❾   BLANC ❼

G NEVILLE ❽   SILVESTRE ❺

VERON ❼ P NEVILLE ❼

BECKHAM ❼   GIGGS ❻

VAN NISTELROOY ❾   SCHOLES ❼

BEATTIE   ORMEROD

MARSDEN

A SVENSSON   OAKLEY   FERNANDES

BRIDGE   M SVENSSON   LUNDEKVAM   DODD ◻

NIEMI

United Subs Solskjaer ❼ for Silvestre (68 mins), Forlan ❽ for P Neville (79), O'Shea ❼ for Van Nistelrooy (87) **Saints Subs** Delap for Ormerod (75 mins), Delgado for Marsden (88)

MATCH STATS

MANCHESTER UNITED		SOUTHAMPTON
57%	POSSESSION	43%
3	SHOTS ON TARGET	3
10	SHOTS OFF TARGET	6
10	CORNERS	2
12	FOULS CONCEDED	18
0	BOOKINGS	1
0	RED CARDS	0

United star man ★

Ruud van Nistelrooy A welcome return

Diego does it again!

> "It's been a great week. I was delighted to score last week, but to get the winner was even better. Hopefully there will be more to come"
>
> DIEGO FORLAN

GOOD THINGS COME TO THOSE WHO WAIT. AND FOR DIEGO FORLAN THE WAIT WAS LONGER THAN MOST. BUT NOW HE SEEMS TO BE MAKING UP FOR LOST TIME.

WHILE ONLY 11 MINUTES on the pitch as a substitute might not warrant Forlan earning a Man of the Match award, there's no doubting he does win the prize for the best appearance by a United player without a shirt on since Giggsy's blitzing run in the FA Cup semi-final against Arsenal in '99 cued the mayhem that would eventually lead us to Treble glory.

The scenes after our late winner against a resilient and impressive Southampton side might not have matched those at Villa Park, but it was a bouncing Old Trafford at the finale all the same.

Too often this season we've expected a United winner in the closing stages only to falter and fail. Today the saviour came in the form of a much-maligned striker. His critics may still reserve their overall judgement but nobody can begrudge him this day. He has a healthy work ethic and the team's unadulterated delight as his powerful 85th minute curling shot hit the back of the Southampton net showed how much they've taken to him.

The nervy jitters that have beset our season so far persisted here, as another side came to Old Trafford thinking they stood a chance against us. How times change. Returning to a 'Fortress Old Trafford' mentality is crucial. But it was pleasing to see an entertaining, attack-minded match played out by both sides.

With all the theories and criticisms that habitually surround a United side that has not yet found top gear, there has been little attention paid to the way our defence has improved in such a short space of time. From our Achilles heel to our backbone in little under a year. We look composed and confident moving forward from the back these days and Rio made several excellent runs. It's just like watching Brazil.

Phil Neville again showed impressive form – and his kissing of the shirt after his goal is always nice to see – and Fabien once again kept his eye on the ball to save the day from a good James Beattie attempt. Yet the feeling remained that the return of Ruud was the biggest difference. He chased everything, he led the line superbly, and most of all he gave the side a much-needed confidence.

Welcome back Van the Man. **BC**

THE TEAMS

CARROLL ⑧

MAY ⑦   FERDINAND ⑥

G NEVILLE ⑥   O'SHEA ⑦

BECKHAM ⑥ ☐   P NEVILLE ⑥ ☐

FORLAN ⑥   FORTUNE ⑤

SOLSKJAER ⑥   NARDIELLO ⑥

DICKOV   SCOWCROFT

DAVIDSON   IMPEY

ROGERS   STEWART   IZZET   SINCLAIR

ELLIOT   HEATH

WALKER

United Subs Scholes ⑥ for P Neville (59), Veron ⑥ for Fortune (65), Richardson ⑦ for Nardiello (74) **Leicester Subs** Summerbee for Elliott (51), Stevenson for Rogers (81), Benjamin for Dickov (81)

MATCH STATS

MANCHESTER UNITED		LEICESTER CITY
56%	POSSESSION	44%
5	SHOTS ON TARGET	2
6	SHOTS OFF TARGET	5
5	CORNERS	6
11	FOULS CONCEDED	16
2	BOOKINGS	3
0	RED CARDS	0

United star man ⭐

Roy Carroll Calm and competent when called upon

Manchester United   BECKHAM (80 PEN), RICHARDSON (90)
Leicester City

2
0

WED 6 NOVEMBER 02 ◆ 8PM ◆ OLD TRAFFORD ◆ ATT: 47,848 ◆ WC 3RD ROUND ◆ REF: C FOY ◆ ENTERTAINMENT: ⭘⭘⭘⭘⭘

Is it a bird? Is it a plane? No, it's Keiran Richardson's career taking off

United progress in Worth-a-go Cup

> **"Keiran is a brave little lad and put his head among the flying boots and bodies to score"**
>
> SIR ALEX FERGUSON

AT THE END OF THE GAME, LEICESTER CITY MANAGER MICKY ADAMS BEMOANED THE LATE PENALTY DECISION AWARDED AGAINST ANDY IMPEY, CLAIMING THE GAME 'HUNG ON IT'.

THOSE OF US AT THE OPPOSITE END from the challenge saw a push (naturally), but those nearer the action, including Sir Alex, thought it was a 'bit soft'. Whatever, it saved us from another 30 minutes of this nonsense that parades as a major cup competition, so thank goodness for referee Foy.

The 48,000 die-hards who turned up to witness 'fireworks' were not disappointed for in the sky above us we were treated to a display from Old Trafford locals who didn't let the fact that a cup tie was taking place down the road spoil their Guy Fawkes celebrations. That however was it, for on the pitch, bar the first 15 seconds, this game was dull.

Leicester are one of the pacesetters in the First Division. They are also in deep financial trouble, so we expected a performance far better than the one they produced. Even a below-par United display was good enough to send them packing.

Before the game, Sir Alex Ferguson made all the right noises as far as the Worthington Cup committee are concerned, claiming this was a cup tie he not only wanted to win, but definitely would be victorious in. 16 years to the day, 'Big' Ron Atkinson lost the United job because a defeat in this competition away at Southampton was deemed to be the final straw. We've come a long way in that time.

So were those who doubted Fergie's words surprised when, at around the hour mark, Scholes and Veron came on to ensure the game didn't go to extra time?

David Beckham must have had the week from hell, taking into account the kidnap threats to his wife and children. Once again, though, he stood tall and took responsibility for his team after the 'soft' push on Ole saw us awarded a penalty. The guy grows in my admiration all the time. No soft options for our Becks.

With the match virtually over, it was nice to see young Kieran Richardson bag his first goal for the first team. United fans like to see big-money signings arriving on the scene at Old Trafford, but we love nothing more than a homegrown player making it to the very top. Let's hope he's next to fall into that illustrious category. **SB**

Manchester City   ANELKA (5), GOATER 2 (26, 50)   **3**
Manchester United   SOLSKJAER (8)   **1**

SAT 9 NOVEMBER 02 ◆ 12.15PM ◆ MAINE ROAD ◆ ATT: 34,649 ◆ PREMIERSHIP ◆ REF: P DURKIN ◆ ENTERTAINMENT: ○○○○○

If you don't want to relive this debacle... look away now

Inadequate, passionless, unacceptable

THE DERBY DAY HIGHLIGHT FOR SOME REDS INSIDE MAINE ROAD'S CONTRASTING MISH-MASH OF STANDS CAME WHEN A FLAG WAS UNFURLED IN CITY'S KIPPAX STREET STAND WHICH READ: 'MANCHESTER IS RED'.

IT WAS TRULY AMUSING TO SEE SO many clueless Blues pass the banner above their heads. It could have been a fitting prelude to United's final visit to Maine Road but, instead, it offered a limp high point on a terrible afternoon.

Even now, the day after this debacle, I'm still fuming and feel cheated at the inadequate and passionless performance by the players of Manchester United. United fans have not had to deal with a Derby defeat since 1989. Under Sir Alex, we've been blessed by consistency and triumph against City, but the 3–1 of 2002 was as painful as the 5–1 of '89. It really was that bad.

City were a goal up after five minutes, Nicolas Anelka the scorer after he hustled Rio Ferdinand off a poor ball from Phil Neville. Ole Gunnar Solskjaer equalised three minutes later with a routine finish and for a while, United looked the better team. Then, in the 26th minute, Shaun 'The Goat' Goater robbed Gary Neville of possession and scored City's second, a piece of defending which ensured Neville was cheered ironically by Blues for the rest of the debacle.

Anelka could, and should, have made it 3–1 when he was put in

12 UNITED AFFORDED CITY A DOZEN SHOTS AT GOAL DURING THIS GAME

Schmeichel: probably a bit busier these days

MATCH STATS

MANCHESTER CITY		MANCHESTER UNITED
42%	POSSESSION	58%
5	SHOTS ON TARGET	5
5	SHOTS OFF TARGET	4
0	CORNERS	9
14	FOULS CONCEDED	16
1	BOOKINGS	2
0	RED CARDS	0

United star man

Paul Scholes Showed the commitment others lacked

SHOTS	1
SHOTS ON TARGET	0
PASSES	79
PASS COMPLETION %	94%
TACKLES	3
DRIBBLES	2
FOULS	2

What the papers said...

one-on-one with Barthez but it was Goater who eventually scored City's third, five minutes after half-time. United were briefly stirred, but appeared devoid of both the quality and inspiration to turn the game – and it's naïve to blame the deficiencies solely on injuries. Ryan Giggs came close to scoring, and John O'Shea missed a sitter but City were worthy victors.

This defeat wasn't a freak one. It had been coming. What concerns me most is how quickly United have slipped from a team that won the Premiership at a canter in 2001 to a side that have looked utterly unconvincing all of this season and throughout much of last. I genuinely fear for the outcome when United play a top-class side.

There are only so many excuses that Sir Alex and the United players can offer before the fans' patience wears thin. Something is clearly wrong, and the derby result merely confirmed the fact to United fans who are becoming bored and frustrated at the current situation. Strong words, but the truth. **AM**

> "We committed stupid errors. The players have had a bollocking in there and rightly so"
>
> SIR ALEX FERGUSON

CHAPTER THREE

THE
FIGHTBACK

A FTER MAINE ROAD United lay in fifth place on 22 points, seven behind Arsenal and 10 adrift of leaders Liverpool. Talk of having the appetite for the fight wouldn't do any more for United fans who wanted to see proof on the pitch. But with a tough sequence of games coming up and Beckham, Keane and Butt all injured, United's prospects looked bleak. So it fell to the unsung heroes of the United squad to help lift the remaining stars out of a depressing rut. Step forward Diego, Phil, Quinton and co...

Wednesday 13 November
BAYER LEVERKUSEN (H)
CHAMPIONS LEAGUE PHASE ONE

Sunday 17 November
WEST HAM UNITED (A)
PREMIERSHIP

Saturday 23 November
NEWCASTLE UNITED (H)
PREMIERSHIP

Tuesday 26 November
FC BASEL (A)
CHAMPIONS LEAGUE PHASE TWO

Sunday 1 December
LIVERPOOL (A)
PREMIERSHIP

Saturday 4 December
BURNLEY (A)
WORTHINGTON CUP RD 4

Saturday 7 December
ARSENAL (H)
PREMIERSHIP

Wednesday 11 December
DEPORTIVO (H)
CHAMPIONS LEAGUE PHASE TWO

Saturday 14 December
WEST HAM UNITED (H)
PREMIERSHIP

Tuesday 17 December
CHELSEA (H)
WORTHINGTON CUP RD 5

Sunday 22 December
BLACKBURN ROVERS (A)
PREMIERSHIP

Thursday 26 December
MIDDLESBROUGH (A)
PREMIERSHIP

Saturday 28 December
BIRMINGHAM CITY (H)
PREMIERSHIP

Manchester United
VERON (42), VAN NISTELROOY (69)

Bayer Leverkusen

2

0

WED 13 NOV 02 ◆ 7.45PM ◆ OLD TRAFFORD ◆ ATT: 66,185 ◆ CL PHASE ONE ◆ REF: V.HRINAK ◆ ENTERTAINMENT: ⓄⓄⓄⓄⓄ

David shapes up to curl one

THE TEAMS

RICARDO ⑥
BLANC ⑥   FERDINAND ⑥
O'SHEA ⑦   VERON ⑥   FORTUNE ⑥   SILVESTRE ⑦
BECKHAM ⑧   SCHOLES ⑦   GIGGS ⑦
VAN NISTELROOY ⑦

BERBATOV
BRDARIC
BIEROFKA   BABIC   SIMAK   BALLITSCH
ZIVKOVIC   KLEINE   RAMELOW   SEBESCEN
BUTT

United Subs G Neville ⑥ for Blanc (77), Solskjaer ⑥ for Beckham (78), Chadwick ⑥ for Giggs (81)
Leverkusen Subs Franca for Berbatov (62), Dogan for Bierofka (78), Preuss for Balitsch (81)

MATCH STATS

MANCHESTER UNITED		BAYER LEVERKUSEN
52%	POSSESSION	48%
9	SHOTS ON TARGET	3
6	SHOTS OFF TARGET	10
7	CORNERS	5
12	FOULS CONCEDED	13
1	BOOKINGS	3
0	RED CARDS	0

United star man ★
David Beckham Worked hard, played well

United warms a packed Old Trafford on a cold night

"There was hunger and commitment, which is what we wanted to see. In general it was a good performance"

SIR ALEX FERGUSON

THE PRIORITIES OF THIS GAME WERE TWOFOLD: TO FINISH TOP OF CHAMPIONS LEAGUE GROUP F AND FOR THE PLAYERS TO SHOW SOME FIGHT AFTER THE DEBACLE AT MAINE ROAD.

THE DERBY DEFEAT WAS BEING FELT hard. Anger had overtaken disappointment and the recriminations in the media, on the fan websites and in the pubs before the game continued – the consensus of opinion being that the team had given a lacklustre performance that had let the supporters down (not to mention themselves).

A good display was called for and though this match effectively meant little, apart from a more favourable

draw for the second phase, United fans wanted to see some effort. In fact, the effort was more important than the display and result.

With no Fabien Barthez, Gary Neville or brother Phil, there were starts for Ricardo, O'Shea and Fortune. Fergie had clearly rung the changes as had mad-haired Leverkusen boss Toppmöller, who rested many of his senior stars. Despite the personnel missing from the match, the game kept the fans' attention and contained the required level of application from the United players. Beckham in particular working hard.

Ricardo's first action of the night resulted in him conceding a penalty, which he duly watched dispatched over the bar towards row 'Z' by Simak. From there United grew in confidence and, through one of Saturday's perceived 'culprits', they took the lead. Following a neat

move, Seba Veron chipped the ball up a yard in front of himself and volleyed a shot into the bottom corner of Butt's net (that's their Butt, not ours, obviously).

In the second half United continued to create chances and the lively Germans also had opportunities. It wasn't the greatest game you've ever seen, lacking the cut and thrust of a match that really meant something. However, a morale-boosting win was called for and that's what the fans were assured of when a Veron pass was touched on by Scholes and tucked away by Van Nistelrooy. It was his tenth of the campaign – not bad for someone supposedly struggling in his second season.

It didn't make up for the defeat against City at Maine Road, but it was a step in the right direction and at least assured us a better draw in the Champions League. **PD**

THE TEAMS

BARTHEZ **6**

O'SHEA **7**   BROWN **7**   BLANC **6**   SILVESTRE **6**

VERON **7**   SCHOLES **7**   FORTUNE **7**   GIGGS **7**

VAN NISTELROOY **7**   SOLSKJAER **7**

DEFOE   DI CANIO

SINCLAIR   CISSE   CARRICK   COLE

WINTERBURN   DAILLY   PEARCE   SCHEMMEL

JAMES

No substitutes used

MATCH STATS

WEST HAM UNITED		MANCHESTER UNITED
50%	POSSESSION	50%
1	SHOTS ON TARGET	5
8	SHOTS OFF TARGET	9
10	CORNERS	6
14	FOULS CONCEDED	16
2	BOOKINGS	1
0	RED CARDS	0

United star man ★

Ryan Giggs Provided a constant threat

West Ham United DEFOE (86) **1**
Manchester United VAN NISTELROOY (38) **1**

SUN 17 NOV 02 ◆ 4.05PM ◆ UPTON PARK ◆ ATT: 35,049 ◆ FA PREMIERSHIP ◆ REF: M HALSEY ◆ ENTERTAINMENT: ●●●○○

Was Ruud's goal offside? Do we care?

Another hammer blow

LIES, DAMN LIES AND STATISTICS. THE PHRASE WAS NEVER MORE APT THAN FOR UNITED'S RECORD AT UPTON PARK.

READING THE SUNDAY NEWSPAPERS as we trundled down the M6, it appeared that the land of jellied eels and bubble-blowing had been a happy hunting ground for us recently.

Fact: United are yet to lose at Upton Park in the Premiership. True, but in this fixture in the last seven years we have lost two league titles, surrendered a couple of two-goal leads and even when we have come out on top, the games have been nerve-wracking affairs. So, the fact that West Ham had yet to win at home this season was more of a cause for concern than confidence among a United support still reeling from the Maine Road horror show.

The anxiety was increased by news of the latest additions to the increasingly popular treatment room club. It was a case of one out, two in as Wes Brown's return was countered by injury blows to David Beckham and Gary Neville.

However, the injuries meant that Ole Solskjaer could resume his partnership with Ruud van Nistelrooy up front. The tactic seemed to bring more movement and purpose to United's attacks with both players certainly enjoying more space than in recent weeks.

Offside decisions, however, were destined to decide the game. West Ham were denied a goal in the first half and United's eventual opener was one the pundits are still debating. While, no doubt, the active/inactive, phase one/phase two debate raged inside the TV studios, the 1–0 scoreline was all that mattered to the travelling Reds.

> "We always have interesting games against West Ham and maybe they deserved their reward. But they have to thank the linesman for their goal"
>
> SIR ALEX FERGUSON

The second half was semi-predictable, typical of Upton Park and of this season. Despite dominating possession, a ruthless streak to make sure of a second goal and finish the game was lacking. Unfortunately the consequences were inevitable.

The warning signs were there. Jermaine Defoe had threatened for most of the game, missing numerous chances and looking lively throughout. A lob over Barthez which landed on top of the bar was followed by what few would deny was a deserved equaliser. Five minutes from time the ball again fell to Defoe, his clear offside position was ignored, and he slotted home.

Desperate attacking from United followed, but David James pulled off two fantastic saves at the death. Two points dropped and with back-to-back games against Liverpool and Arsenal approaching, it's looking like nothing less than six points will do. **RS**

Manchester United
SCHOLES (25), VAN NISTELROOY 3 (38, 45, 53), SOLSKJAER (55)

Newcastle United
BERNARD (35), SHEARER (52), BELLAMY (75)

5

3

SAT 23 NOV 02 ◆ 12.15PM ◆ OLD TRAFFORD ◆ ATT: 67,619 ◆ FA PREMIERSHIP ◆ REF: S DUNN ◆ ENTERTAINMENT: ✪✪✪✪✪

United turned over the Geordies in style

THE TEAMS

BARTHEZ 7

BROWN 9   BLANC 7

O'SHEA 8   SILVESTRE 9

SCHOLES 9   FORTUNE 8

SOLSKJAER 8 ■   FORLAN 7   GIGGS 7

VAN NISTELROOY 9 ■

BELLAMY   SHEARER

BERNARD   JENAS

SPEED   DYER

HUGHES   GRIFFIN

DABIZAS   O'BRIEN

GIVEN

United Subs Richardson 8 for Van Nistelrooy (64), Roche 7 for Blanc (70), Veron 7 for Forlan (80)

Newcastle United Subs Solano for Bernard (72)

MATCH STATS

MANCHESTER UNITED		NEWCASTLE UNITED
52%	POSSESSION	48%
9	SHOTS ON TARGET	6
3	SHOTS OFF TARGET	3
2	CORNERS	8
17	FOULS CONCEDED	9
2	BOOKINGS	2
0	RED CARDS	0

United star man ⭐

Paul Scholes Run of great form continues

A tale of two knights

> "Five goals against Newcastle tells you we have reached a different level from the rest of the season. That has been waiting to happen for some time and provides great encouragement to us all"
>
> SIR ALEX FERGUSON

THE PRE-MATCH BUILD-UP CENTRED ON BOBBY ROBSON JOINING THAT ELITE BAND OF FOOTBALLING SIRS. BY FULL-TIME, THE TALK WAS OF THE RETURN OF UNITED'S CLINICAL SELVES.

WHILE THE MEDIA VULTURES HAVE continued to hover above Old Trafford with their crisis talk, Reds know that you never judge a season during our seemingly annual autumnal difficulties and Robson himself was quick to identify this. After receiving a smacking on the shoulders from the royal sword, he took time out at Buck House to praise Sir Alex, suggesting that talk of United's demise was premature.

His words proved prophetic as

United came out of the blocks looking confident and, crucially, with belief. While Reds have seen too much happen this season already to regard this fixture as anything but a sticky one, there was something in our early play that differed from our previous home fixtures this season. Our passing and movement was destructive, our play quick one-touch football that saw us move from defence to attack in seconds. The United of old, indeed.

There was however a bizarre, somewhat crazy aura to the whole game. We dominated and kept possession well, yet somehow managed to concede three goals (at one stage they represented the Magpies' only three attempts on goal), one of which was a Seaman-type loop over Barthez. It was placed – or should that be misdirected – with such precision that you would have needed all three of our goalies

on the line to have stopped it. For another, Bellamy's, we adopted a Keystone Cops attitude to ridding the ball from the box.

But they are slight criticisms from a very good afternoon's work. The fans responded in kind and, rarely for an early kick-off, at times Old Trafford was bouncing, with the ditties aimed at their Number Nine always a particular joy to hear.

When the team play this well, it's always hard to pick out just one man of the match. Ole's goal (and the through-ball leading to it) thrilled, Silvestre again looked positive but Scholes earnt his plaudits with an aggressive display. Truly one of Europe's best.

Our 30-year undefeated home record against Newcastle remains intact, and the day was further buoyed with later news of defeats to Liverpool and Arsenal. How quickly things can turn around. **BC**

THE TEAMS

ZUBERBUHLER

M.YAKIN   ZWYSSIG

HAAS   CANTALUPPI   ATOUBA

ERGIC   CHIPPERFIELD

GIMINEZ   H. YAKIN   ROSSI

VAN NISTELROOY **9**

GIGGS **6**   SCHOLES **7**   SOLSKJAER **7**

FORTUNE **6**   VERON **6**

SILVESTRE **7**   P NEVILLE **6**

O'SHEA **6**   BROWN **7**

BARTHEZ **6**

FC Basel Subs Tum for Chipperfield (73), Duruz for Rossi (85), Barberis for Ergic (85)
United Subs Forlan **7** for Richardson (73), May for Forlan (89), Chadwick for Solskjaer (89)

MATCH STATS

FC BASEL		MANCHESTER UNITED
48%	POSSESSION	52%
5	SHOTS ON TARGET	5
7	SHOTS OFF TARGET	5
9	CORNERS	5
9	FOULS CONCEDED	13
2	BOOKINGS	3
0	RED CARDS	0

United star man ⭐

Ruud van Nistelrooy Marco van Who?

FC Basel   GIMINEZ (1)   **1**

Manchester United   VAN NISTELROOY (62, 63)   SOLSKJAER (68)   **3**

TUE 26 NOVEMBER 02 ◆ 7.45PM ◆ ST JAKOB PARK ◆ ATT: 35,000 ◆ CL PHASE TWO ◆ REF: IVANOV ◆ ENTERTAINMENT ◆◆◆◆◇

Ruud defied the laws of geometry to score his second

The Ruud van Nistelrooy show!

"YOU'RE NOT BOUNCING ANY MORE," SANG THE 1,600 UNITED FANS TUCKED AWAY IN THE CORNER OF THE ST JAKOB PARK STADIUM. WE'D JUST WITNESSED ANOTHER STRIKING MASTERCLASS FROM OUR FLYING DUTCHMAN.

WHAT BETTER WAY TO WARM UP FOR a trip to Anfield than beating the team that dumped the Scousers out of the Champions League a fortnight earlier?

But the game didn't start too well. By the time I'd found somewhere to stand, United were behind and for an hour it looked like we might lose. However, the mood among the travelling Reds remained optimistic. And why not with a striker of Van Nistelrooy's ability on the pitch?

When he arrived at Old Trafford he was likened to Dutch legend Marco van Basten, but not everyone agreed. Liverpool fans scoffed at the comparison and muttered among themselves the words 'unproven,' 'serious injury' and 'waste of money'. He started by showing what he is capable of in the Charity Shield against them on his debut, and has never looked back. He's had the odd spell where he's failed to score from open play (earlier this season he was supposedly a striker in 'crisis') but no United fan doubted his class.

The faith of the fans was rewarded in Switzerland once again. Following on from his hat-trick against Newcastle, he increased his season's tally by two. The first was a clinical header from close range after an Ole Gunnar Solskjaer cross, which got United back into the game and stopped the Basel fans bouncing, but

> "Ruud's finishing is fantastic. I see him do it every day in training and in matches. He's got a tremendous record for us"
>
> SIR ALEX FERGUSON

the best was to come. 90 seconds after his equaliser, the Dutchman put United ahead in the game. It was a goal to rival any scored by Van Basten. Collecting a loose ball in the corner of the Basel penalty area, Ruud turned and ran at two defenders. A succession of body swerves, feints and dummies left him with only the keeper to beat, but from an almost impossibly tight angle. No problem for United's number 10 though, who simply curled the ball in off the far post. He'd single-handedly turned the match on its head.

Once our wonder striker set up Ole for the third the three points were sealed. It was a perfect start for United Champions League Phase Two. There were good performances throughout the team but there's no doubting the main man was Ruud van Basten... sorry, Nistelrooy – it's an easy mistake to make. **PD**

Liverpool HYYPIA (82)

Manchester United FORLAN (63, 66)

1
2

SUN 1 DEC 02 ◆ 12.15PM ◆ ANFIELD ◆ ATT: 44,250 ◆ FA PREMIERSHIP ◆ REF: A WILEY ◆ ENTERTAINMENT: ⬤⬤⬤⬤⬤

Two-goal hero Diego meets his adoring fans

THE TEAMS

```
                    DUDEK
          HENCHOZ        HYYPIA
  CARRAGHER      HAMANN           TRAORE
      GERRARD                  MURPHY
                    SMICER
          BAROS              OWEN

              VAN NISTELROOY ❼ ▢
  GIGGS ❼         FORLAN ⑧         SOLSKJAER ⑧
          FORTUNE ❼     SCHOLES ⑧
    O'SHEA ⑧                      G NEVILLE ⑧
        SILVESTRE ⑧   ▢  BROWN ⑧
                 BARTHEZ ⑧
```

Liverpool Subs Heskey for Baros (59),
Diouf for Smicer (70), Riise for Traore (78)
United Subs P Neville ⑥ for Fortune (81),
May for Van Nistelrooy (88), Stewart for Forlan (89)

MATCH STATS

LIVERPOOL		MANCHESTER UNITED
55%	POSSESSION	45%
5	SHOTS ON TARGET	4
5	SHOTS OFF TARGET	0
5	CORNERS	2
14	FOULS CONCEDED	13
1	BOOKINGS	4
0	RED CARDS	0

United star man ⭐

Diego Forlan Uruguay... Scousers cry... it rhymes!

Anfield romp

"The breaks are starting to come our way!"

SIR ALEX FERGUSON

WE WERE WELCOMED INTO ANFIELD BY THE SIGHT OF THE KOP HOLDING UP BOARDS PROCLAIMING 'THIS IS ANFIELD'.

AS WE HAD SUCCESSFULLY MADE OUR way down the M62, it was presumably there to remind Liverpool's out-of-towners that they, dressed in their jesters hats and waving silly big flags, had indeed arrived at their destination in, and around, the McDonalds stand.

Just what Ronald would have said about the game, however, is anybody's guess – for by the final whistle it was the Liverpool keeper who looked the clown more than the Kop's more famous patron.

If the Manchester derby left us feeling betrayed, then this match was the first real chance for the players to show us what pulling on the Red shirt means. They didn't disappoint. Right from the first crunching tackle of the game, we saw a display of passion, guts, steely determination, and not least some pretty good football. The game itself might not have been a classic, but the will to win and the spirit we long for was there for all to see.

With five defeats on the bounce to Liverpool, the half-time deadlock looked ominous. We were clearly the best team, but one slip-up could cost us, and we were aware of it. So when just after the hour an innocuous-looking header was steered back to Dudek in the Liverpool goal, you'd have been forgiven for averting your eyes from the early winter's sun to check just how long was left. Fortunately, though, Diego didn't do likewise, and in the blink of an eye we took a deserved lead.

With our tails up and Liverpool shell-shocked, the next goal was always going to be the clincher, and when Scholes broke up another Liverpool move, surged forward and passed to Ryan who fed Diego just three minutes later, our media-maligned hero thumped the ball past Dudek to double the lead.

It wouldn't be United not to give us a few heart-stopping moments, and after Hyypia had poked one home, we wondered if our luck would once again run out. But while one keeper was having a nightmare, the one that mattered wasn't. Fabien's save from Hamann's piledriver was one of his best in a United shirt.

The players were hammered by us fans after the derby defeat. After this victory we therefore should praise them as lavishly. The pain of the derby might not have gone, but it certainly felt better as the final whistle blew. **SB**

THE TEAMS

BERESFORD

DAVIS   GNOHERE

WEST   BRANCH

COOK   BRISCOE

WELLER   BLAKE

LITTLE   TAYLOR

VAN NISTELROOY 7   FORLAN 8

PUGH 6   CHADWICK 7

STEWART 6   O'SHEA 7

SILVESTRE 7   P NEVILLE 7

MAY 7   BROWN 8

CARROLL 7

Burnley Subs Grant for Cook (57), Papadopoulos for Briscoe, Moore for Gnohere (72)
United Subs Solskjaer 7 for Van Nistelrooy (45), Scholes 8 for Stewart (58), Giggs 7 for Forlan (76)

United star man ⭐

Diego Forlan He's on a roll

Burnley   0

Manchester United   FORLAN (35), SOLSKJAER (65)   2

WED 3 DECEMBER 02 ◆ 8PM ◆ TURF MOOR ◆ ATT: 22,034 ◆ WORTHINGTON CUP 4TH RND ◆ REF: N BARRY ◆ ENTERTAINMENT: ●●●●○

Ole notches United's second goal of the night

United progress in Worth-a-go Cup!

THE WORTHINGTON CUP HAS BEEN SNEERED AT AND GIVEN A CRUEL 'WORTHLESS CUP' MONIKER BY PREMIERSHIP SUPPORTERS, INCLUDING REDS, IN RECENT YEARS.

CERTAINLY, THE COMPETITION HAS hardly been at the top of Sir Alex's trophy list, with United usually represented by inexperienced players who looked like they wouldn't need a razor in their Vuitton wash bags.

This season has been different though. Stronger United line-ups have meant that the competition hasn't been limited to a solo 90-minute exercise and the merits of the competition have been tangible, as Burnley away in the fourth round illustrated. A hefty 4,000-plus ticket

allocation at an impressively redeveloped ground that had not been visited by many Reds resulted in a belting local cup-tie played in a cracking atmosphere.

Burnley's 88,000 population makes the town the smallest to have hosted top-flight football on a consistent basis, and while the days of Burnley FC playing at the highest level are long gone, the recent revival under Manager Stan Ternant has seen the Clarets establish themselves as a first division side once again. In doing so, they have lifted spirits in a depressed and aesthetically-challenged town normally associated with negative media headlines relating to local right-wing politics.

The atmosphere was rocking in the United end. A chant of: "You're just a small town in Blackburn", was intended to rile the locals who despise their neighbours to the west. It did. Chants of: "Diego, he came

> "You can see the confidence those goals at Liverpool have given him. Now people are seeing Diego at his best"
>
> SIR ALEX FERGUSON

from Uruguay, he made the Scousers cry", celebrated Forlan's Anfield brace and, appropriately, it was the man from Montevideo who made the difference for United at Turf Moor.

The first half was evenly matched, fast-paced and goalless until United's man of the moment slid in his sixth of the season from a John O'Shea pass on 35 minutes. United were easily stronger in the second period and Danny Pugh had three good chances to score before half-time substitute Ole Solskjaer made it 2–0 on 65 minutes after excellent work from Luke Chadwick down the right.

United looked more than capable of scoring again, but it was the announcement that a Burnley player, Glen Little, had been made man of the match that brought the final entertainment. "Fergie, sign him on", sang Reds ironically.

And who said that we couldn't enjoy the Worthington Cup? **AM**

Manchester United VERON (22), SCHOLES (73) 2
Arsenal 0

SAT 7 DECEMBER 02 ◆ 12.15PM ◆ OLD TRAFFORD ◆ ATT: 67,650 ◆ FA PREMIERSHIP ◆ REF: D GALLAGHER ◆ ENTERTAINMENT ✪✪✪✪✪

Phil Neville: absolutely outstanding against Vieira in midfield

A lesson in outgunning the Gooners

THE JOYOUS REACTIONS OF REDS ON WARWICK ROAD AFTER
THE GAME TOLD ITS OWN STORY. NEWS OF UNITED'S DEMISE
HAS BEEN SOMEWHAT PREMATURE...

FIVE WINS ON THE BOUNCE HAVE
seen the club reinvigorate their
season only two weeks after Fergie's
stuttering team faced a daunting
series of matches that could have all
but ended it.

No-one expects this team to win
every game but it's only right for
supporters to demand that highly-
paid players consistently apply the
maximum effort. This tremendous

result was evidence of what can be
achieved when the team displays the
right level of application and
determination. No-one epitomised
the renewed spirit coursing through
the side more than Phil Neville,
whose dogged performance
alongside Veron allowed the pair the
unlikely privilege of midfield
superiority over Vieira and Silva. As
at Anfield the previous week, a few

heavy challenges early in the game
set the tone, showed the opposition
this team meant business and
determined who won the right to be
able to play the football as the
match progressed.

Equally busy and effective were
Scholes and Solskjaer, defending
high up the pitch. Meanwhile
United's ever more solid defence
with Wes Brown and Mikael
Silvestre at the core allowed Henry
and Pires only two early chances
(which they duly squandered).

Arsenal's bright passing

9 PHIL NEVILLE MADE NINE TACKLES, THREE TIMES AS MANY AS ARSENAL MIDFIELDER PATRICK VIEIRA

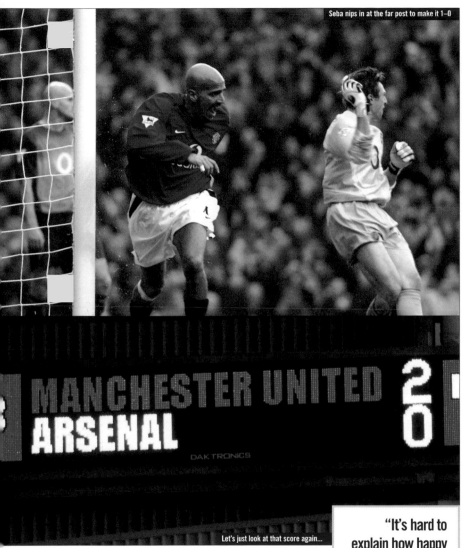

Seba nips in at the far post to make it 1–0

MANCHESTER UNITED 2
ARSENAL 0
DAK TRONICS

Let's just look at that score again...

movements early on gradually disappeared the more they were harried and disrupted and with the red shirts allowing fewer and fewer options to the Arsenal players, the alarming unforced errors from last season's champions became more and more frequent.

Veron's strike for the first goal was celebrated as few others have been at Old Trafford of late and was just reward for the superb vocal support provided by the fans. By the time Paul Scholes added a second, Arsenal were a beaten side; their fire and spirit extinguished.

In the ongoing battle for domestic supremacy this defeat will hit Arsenal and Wenger hard. United have dragged themselves back into the title race and, with the likes of Keane, Beckham and Ferdinand still to return, they look well set to remain there. And remain there they should, but only if the lesson that application is all remains to the fore. It's a lesson you can be sure Wenger will be ramming home long before our next meeting. **JPO**

"It's hard to explain how happy we are because we're so satisfied. Now we know we're back on track and well into the fight for the title"

OLE GUNNAR SOLSKJAER

Manchester United 2
VAN NISTELROOY 2 (7, 55)

Deportivo La Coruña 0

WED 13 DECEMBER 02 ◆ 7.45PM ◆ OLD TRAFFORD ◆ ATT: 67,014 ◆ CL PHASE TWO ◆ REF: T HAUGE ◆ ENTERTAINMENT: ⭐⭐⭐⭐⭐

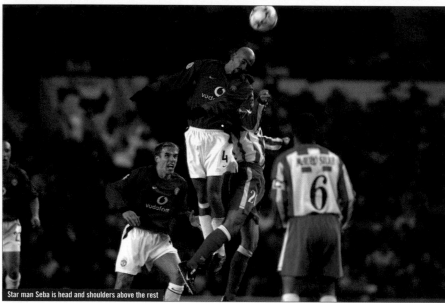

Star man Seba is head and shoulders above the rest

THE TEAMS

BARTHEZ 8
BROWN 8   SILVESTRE 7
G NEVILLE 7   O'SHEA 7
VERON 9   P NEVILLE 7
SOLSKJAER 7   GIGGS 7
SCHOLES 8
VAN NISTELROOY 8

VALERON   MAKAAY
AMAVISCA   VICTOR
SERGIO
CAPDEVILA   MAURO SILVA   SCALONI
ROMERO   CESAR
JUANMI

United Subs Beckham 6 for P Neville (81), Forlan 5 for O'Shea (81), Richardson 5 for Van Nistelrooy (88)
Depor Subs Tristan for Amavisca (46), Luque for Victor (75)

MATCH STATS

MANCHESTER UNITED		DEPORTIVO
48%	POSSESSION	52%
11	SHOTS ON TARGET	4
6	SHOTS OFF TARGET	6
5	CORNERS	6
17	FOULS CONCEDED	7
2	BOOKINGS	1
0	RED CARDS	0

United star man ⭐
Seba Veron Another fine Euro display

Red hot United warm up a cold Manchester night

> "In the first half we had to concentrate hard, but in the second we improved and did really well. Obviously Ruud's second goal killed it, but it was a very good team performance"
>
> SIR ALEX FERGUSON

I'LL BE HONEST WITH YOU. I MISSED THE FIRST GOAL. I DON'T DO IT VERY OFTEN. IT HAPPENED AT SELHURST PARK IN 1996 WHEN BECKHAM DECIDED TO SHOOT AND SCORE FROM THE HALFWAY LINE WITH ONLY INJURY TIME REMAINING. BUT OTHER THAN THAT I RARELY MISS UNITED SCORING...

EXCEPT TONIGHT, THAT IS. I STAYED in the warmth of the pub for 10 minutes too long, then got stuck in a queue outside the Stretford End and was using the facilities when a roar went up for Ruud's first goal, a powerful header following an inch-perfect cross from Scholes.

By the time I sat down the public address system had announced Ruud as the scorer and the Stretford End had embarked on several verses of his song. I wasn't the only one to miss the Dutchman's 17th (19th if you include qualifiers) Champions League goal for the Reds others too were finding their seats. None seemed very

worried. Perhaps they too were confident that United would score again and we'd be able to go home with at least one memory to cherish.

For most of the first half United seemed content to let Deportivo come at them. This wasn't the imagined defensive attitude that Arsene Whinger waffled on about, this was just a good team being pushed back by another team searching for an equaliser. Several times the Spanish side went close to getting their goal, and several times they were denied by stout defending and a couple of tremendous saves by Fabien Barthez.

In the second half United got the upper hand again. Giggs caused problems for Deportivo down the left, Scholes was excellent and Solskjaer continued his impressive form on the right wing.

The second goal, or first to some, came after Scholes' shot was parried by Juanmi in the Spaniards' goal. Ole battled for the rebound and squared it. Who should be there to score? Only the best striker in Europe. Ruud smashed the ball home. Game over. It was nothing less than the Reds deserved with two penalty shouts, including one absolute dead cert, denied by a poor referee and two goals disallowed (possibly rightly).

Near the end David Beckham got a run out and the Stretford End, noting his haircut, piped up with, "One Rod Stewart, there's only one Rod Stewart." It was a humourous end to an enjoyable night, even for those who missed the first goal. **PD**

THE TEAMS

BARTHEZ **7**

G NEVILLE **7**   BROWN **7**   SILVESTRE **7**   O'SHEA **8**

SOLSKJAER **7**   VERON **7**   P NEVILLE **7**   GIGGS **7**

VAN NISTELROOY **6**   SCHOLES **7**

PEARCE   DEFOE

SINCLAIR   COLE   CARRICK   LOMAS

MINTO   DAILLY   REPKA   SCHEMMEL

JAMES

United Subs Beckham **6** for Solskjaer (46),
Forlan **6** for O'Shea (73), Blanc **6** for Scholes (73)
West Ham Subs Moncur for Lomas (85), Breen for Minto (89)

MATCH STATS

MANCHESTER UNITED		WEST HAM UNITED
53%	POSSESSION	47%
8	SHOTS ON TARGET	2
5	SHOTS OFF TARGET	7
7	CORNERS	4
13	FOULS CONCEDED	12
0	BOOKINGS	1
0	RED CARDS	0

United star man ★

John O'Shea Grows with every game

Manchester United
SOLSKJAER (15), VERON (17), SCHEMMEL OG (61)

West Ham United

3
0

SAT 14 DECEMBER 02 ◆ 12.15PM ◆ OLD TRAFFORD ◆ ATT: 67,555 ◆ FA PREMIERSHIP ◆ REF: R STYLES ◆ ENTERTAINMENT: ●●●○○

Dance with me, bro!

Banana skin safely negotiated

THE DAY BEFORE THE GAME, PHIL NEVILLE SUGGESTED THAT THIS MATCH WAS AS IMPORTANT AS ANY THE REDS HAD PLAYED IN THE LAST MONTH, A FACT NOT LOST ON UNITED FANS.

HAVING BEATEN BOTH OF OUR MAIN title rivals in back to back matches, all the good work would have been undone by a defeat at home to West Ham. And make no mistake, that wasn't as ridiculous a prospect as you might imagine, the Hammers having won on their previous two visits.

The opening exchanges indicated that both sides were apparently content to ease their way into the game. Gradually the fluency that has come flooding back into the Reds' play in recent weeks showed itself

again. Full-backs John O'Shea and Gary Neville pushed forward, Veron orchestrated affairs in midfield and Scholes and Van Nistelrooy pulled West Ham's back four all across the pitch. A goal surely had to come?

Sure enough it arrived, via a deflection from a Solskjaer header. The Norwegian has been a revelation on the right wing and showed the value of having a winger with a striker's instinct when freed to push forward by Gary Neville's attacking play. Any fears of this match being a potential banana skin were fading.

West Ham looked lively at times, Jermaine Defoe having a goal wrongly scratched off for offside, but the Reds' defence looked solid. However, it wouldn't have mattered had they scored because United were in expansive mood, carving open the Londoners at will.

The second goal was inevitable, not to mention spectacular. Seba Veron

> "We played some fantastic football in the first half and looked like scoring quite a few"
>
> SIR ALEX FERGUSON

has grown in the absence of Keane, and also been given a chance to take free-kicks in the absence of Beckham. So when the Reds were awarded a free-kick in shooting range, the Stretford End called for "Veron, Veron" to take it. The Argentinian stepped forward and with a swing of his wand-like right foot curled a superb shot over the wall and inside David James' right-hand post. It was a majestic goal from a player finally justifying his transfer fee.

The second half saw Beckham arrive to more chants of "One Rod Stewart" and though he didn't enjoy the best of games, he played a part in United's third goal – Gary Neville eventually seeing his low cross diverted into his own net by Sebastien Schemmel.

With Wes Brown and Silvestre giving a (now) typically strong display at the back, even West Ham's late flourish didn't threaten to take the points away. **PD**

Manchester United FORLAN (80)

Chelsea

1

0

TUE 17 DECEMBER 02 ◆ 8PM ◆ OLD TRAFFORD ◆ ATT: 57,985 ◆ WORTHINGTON CUP ROUND 5 ◆ REF: S BENNETT ◆ ENTERTAINMENT: ●●●○○

These winning goals are becoming a habit for Diego

United reach Worthy Cup semis!

AND SO UNITED MARCH ON INTO THE SEMI-FINALS OF THE LEAGUE CUP AND BEGIN THE NEW YEAR CHALLENGING FOR TROPHIES ON FOUR FRONTS FOR THE FIRST TIME SINCE 1991.

SUCH IS THE CLUB'S RESURGENT interest in the League Cup, almost 58,000 turned up at only two weeks' notice and provided a lively backdrop to an entertaining contest that, despite the air of indifference that so often surrounds the competition, the two teams evidently wanted to win.

It was certainly not a classic match,

UNITED AND CHELSEA MUSTERED JUST SHOTS ON TARGET BETWEEN THEM IN THIS GAME

6

but still highly compelling for those who appreciate the defensive art as much as the offensive. For it was both teams' back lines which excelled here and there was no player more impressive than Mikael Silvestre.

Having finally been given the centre-half role he so cherishes, the Frenchman is making a great case for not returning him to the left, showing the sort of form that emphasised why United were so keen to tie him to the new contract which was announced earlier in the day.

Almost as impressive was Wes

Brown, alongside him yet again despite the return to fitness of Laurent Blanc. Given the excellent understanding Brown and Silvestre have developed in recent games, there's no reason why anyone should disrupt their partnership just yet, even taking into account the imminent return of a certain £30 million summer signing.

With both defences in fine form, few clear chances were created. When Chelsea did find a way through they were consistently denied by Barthez – most notably

Sheasy makes a nuisance of himself in the Chelsea box

MANCHESTER UNITED 1
CHELSEA 0

DAKTRONICS

0:00 MINS

We're through to the semis...

MATCH STATS

MANCHESTER UNITED		CHELSEA
51%	POSSESSION	49%
2	SHOTS ON TARGET	4
6	SHOTS OFF TARGET	7
4	CORNERS	9
8	FOULS CONCEDED	14
1	BOOKINGS	2
0	RED CARDS	0

United star man

Mikael Silvestre Building a strong partnership with Wes

What the papers said...

'Diego Forlan struck 10 minutes from time against Chelsea at Old Trafford to make it eight wins on the bounce for United and send them through to the last four for the first time since 1994.
'The Uruguayan has enjoyed a remarkable turnaround in his fortunes. After failing to find the back of the net last season, he has now scored four times in his last five games.'
David Anderson, Daily Mirror

'Don't let anyone tell you Manchester United aren't serious about winning this competition. This was as serious as it gets. 'And now Sir Alex Ferguson's team are in the semi finals for the first time since 1994. Back then, United were beaten by Aston Villa in the final. But this time they're in the mood to make the Worthington Cup their first trophy of the season.'
Bill Thornton, Daily Star

"The great Worthington Cup gamble was born out of desperation, at a time when his Manchester United team could not afford to treat any competition lightly, but suddenly it is beginning to look like a masterstroke by Sir Alex Ferguson."
Oliver Kay, Times

when acrobatically saving a Hasselbaink special – while in the second half Zola found his way blocked by a stunning recovery tackle from Brown when all set to score. For United, Giggs couldn't quite lob the ball over Cudicini and Scholes was largely restricted to long-range efforts.

In such an evenly balanced match, it was ironic that the hero should again be Diego Forlan, this time without the help of Jerzy Dudek. He'd earlier been so ineffective alongside Scholes that he'd taken to drifting out wide, but when the moment came he was there to pick up Beckham's killer pass and apply a decisive finish.

Minutes later United's semi-final berth could have been assured, but an easier chance for Diego scraped past the post.

No matter, an eighth consecutive win was duly completed and perhaps more importantly given the trials of the past 18 months, United recorded our fifth game in a row without conceding a goal. What a difference a month makes. **JPO**

> "Now we are in the semi-finals we will try and win it"
>
> SIR ALEX FERGUSON

Blackburn Rovers FLITCROFT (40) 1
Manchester United 0

SUN 22 DECEMBER 02 ◆ 2PM ◆ EWOOD PARK ◆ ATT: 30,475 ◆ FA PREMIERSHIP ◆ REF: D ELLERAY ◆ ENTERTAINMENT: ◉◉◉○○

The 'best keeper in the Premiership' thwarts Ruud

Red winning run halted by Rovers

IN A GAME PLAYED IN THE MISERABLE HALF-LIGHT OF A
LANCASHIRE WINTER DAY, UNITED SET OUT TO ADD TO THEIR
EIGHT-MATCH RUN OF CONSECUTIVE VICTORIES.

WITHOUT A WIN AGAINST UNITED in eight years, Blackburn were the underdogs with the bookmakers, but football is seldom so predictable.

Despite the presence of Roy Keane on the United bench after a 26-game absence, the limp atmosphere on three sides of the ground led to a lack of occasion inside Ewood Park.

United were by far the better team in the first period and passed the ball around with the confidence of a team in form. Backed by a highly vocal following of 7,000, who completely outsang the home supporters, Sir Alex's men almost toyed with Blackburn. Chances and openings were created with a series of quick attacking movements, but poor finishing meant the game remained goalless.

At the other end, Barthez was seldom troubled and even a save from a Dunn strike seven minutes before half-time looked more dramatic than it actually was. Two minutes later though, the Frenchman had little chance when Flitcroft half-volleyed a poor clearance through a crowded box. Coming against the run of play, it was also the first goal United had conceded in over eight hours.

Blackburn were more assertive in the second period, taking the game to United with Cole and Yorke troubling our defenders. Luckily, the

BLACKBURN ROVERS BEAT
UNITED DESPITE
MANAGING JUST TWO
SHOTS ON TARGET
2

Rovers goalscorer Flitcroft challenges Scholes

THE TEAMS

FRIEDEL

NEILL   SHORT   TAYLOR   JOHANSSON

DUNN   FLITCROFT   TUGAY   DUFF

YORKE   COLE

VAN NISTELROOY ⑥   FORLAN ⑥

GIGGS ⑥   SOLSKJAER ⑥

P NEVILLE ⑦   SCHOLES ⑦

SILVESTRE ⑥   O'SHEA ⑥

G NEVILLE ⑦ ☐ BROWN ⑥

BARTHEZ ⑥

Blackburn Subs Gillespie for Dunn (55)
United Subs Keane ⑥ for Forlan (69),
Beckham ⑤ for Giggs (70), Blanc ⑤ for P Neville (85)

MATCH STATS

BLACKBURN ROVERS		MANCHESTER UNITED
47%	POSSESSION	53%
2	SHOTS ON TARGET	3
8	SHOTS OFF TARGET	6
7	CORNERS	8
9	FOULS CONCEDED	12
0	BOOKINGS	1
0	RED CARDS	0

KEANE RETURNS... QUIETLY

MINUTES	31
SHOTS	0
PASSES	24
PASS COMPLETION %	76%
TACKLES	0
CLEARANCES	1
FOULS	1

What the papers said...

'United's travelling fans were on their way to singing themselves hoarse but still welcomed back Roy Keane noisily after demanding his return. But even the Irishman's influence can't alter fate. When van Nistelrooy was presented by Scholes with an inviting 67th minute chance, the Dutchman was forced wide by Blackburn keeper Brad Friedel and for once he rushed his shot, defeat became inevitable.'
Stuart Mathieson, MEN

'No sooner had Manchester United been made favourites to go into the new year as Premiership leaders, than they were brought down to earth by a wonderfully determined Blackburn Rovers yesterday. The gap on defending champions Arsenal remains four points.'
William Johnson, Daily Telegraph

United star man ★

Gary Neville In a defence tormented by Cole & Yorke

---

two ex-Reds showed a similar profligacy in front of goal to Van Nistelrooy. In one of several good goalscoring opportunities, Ruud was pressed into a one-on-one with goalkeeper Friedel. The American – the best keeper in the Premiership this season according to many commentators – did well to smother the ball, but Ruud will be disappointed he didn't do better.

When Keane was introduced on 59 minutes, the boos that rang out in the home end were easily eclipsed by the cheers of the Red partisans

in the Darwen End. "Keano, there's only one Keano," came the cry complimented by a large banner reading: "And on the Eighth Day God Created Keane". Neither Keane, nor fellow sub Beckham, could breach Blackburn's defences though and if anything, their introduction confused United's formation.

It was an exciting finish as United interspersed Blackburn's possession by pushing for an equaliser, but it just wasn't going to happen today. **AM**

> **"It was a great performance by us. United are a top team"**
>
> GRAEME SOUNESS

Middlesbrough
BOKSIC (44), NEMETH (48), JOB (85)

Manchester United
GIGGS (60)

3

1

THU 26 DECEMBER 02 ◆ 4PM ◆ RIVERSIDE STADIUM ◆ ATT: 34,673 ◆ FA PREMIERSHIP ◆ REF: G BARBER ◆ ENTERTAINMENT ●●●●○

Master and pupil look on

THE TEAMS

SCHWARZER

EHIOGU   SOUTHGATE

PARNABY   WILSON   QUEUDRUE

GEREMI   GREENING

JOB

NEMETH   BOKSIC

VAN NISTELROOY ⑥

SCHOLES ⑦ ☐

GIGGS ⑥   SOLSKJAER ⑥

VERON ⑧   KEANE ⑥

O'SHEA ⑦   G NEVILLE ⑥

BLANC ⑥   BROWN ⑦ ☐

BARTHEZ ⑥

Boro Subs Wilkshire for Boksic (63),
Maccarone for Nemeth (83)
United Subs Beckham ⑥ for G Neville (72),
Ferdinand ⑥ for O'Shea (83)

MATCH STATS

MIDDLESBROUGH		MANCHESTER UNITED
44%	POSSESSION	56%
4	SHOTS ON TARGET	3
5	SHOTS OFF TARGET	3
5	CORNERS	8
7	FOULS CONCEDED	13
0	BOOKINGS	2
0	RED CARDS	0

United star man ★

Seba Veron His passing and vision went unrewarded

Smothered by the smog monsters

> "Considering the possession that we had, 3–1 is a bad scoreline. We had great possession but we didn't have the concentration to capitalise"
>
> SIR ALEX FERGUSON

IS IT REALLY THE MYSTERY THE PRESS ARE MAKING IT OUT TO BE THAT MIDDLESBROUGH ARE UNABLE TO WIN (OR EVEN SCORE GOALS FOR THAT MATTER) AWAY FROM THE RIVERSIDE?

ANY SIDE MANAGED/COACHED BY Steve McClaren is going to struggle if his side goes a goal behind. After all, invention, the mother of necessity, is not his strong point. However, if they get a goal up – particularly at home in front of their choreographed fans in their plastic dream of the soulless 'nouveau' stadium they've built in the middle of nowhere – they're going to get the breaks from time to time. It's just unfortunate that today turned out to be one of those times.

Middlesbrough's counter-attacking football is quick and skilful, and at times quite pretty. However, the fact that they only really created chances either side of half-time and once right at the end of the game when every United player but Barthez was laying siege on Schwarzer's goal says a lot. For if an equaliser had come during the lengthy period of play when United enjoyed over 75 per cent of ball possession, then it would have been far more deserved and far less cruel on us than the eventual result.

That we didn't score was caused by a mixture of bad luck, poor refereeing and questionable decision-making from our strike-force. Coming on the back of the setback at Blackburn, however, it was more than just disappointing after fighting our way back into the title race with superb wins over last year's first- and second-placed teams.

However, there were some positives to take from the game: the continued excellent form of Wes Brown, ditto Seba Veron (he was our only real creative threat and his passing and vision were superb) and last but not least, the return of our skipper Roy Keane for his first full 90 minutes in four months. If we are to wrestle the title back from Highbury then we'll need the heart of our side back for the rest of the season, and beating as strongly as ever.

Come tomorrow morning, Ruud van Nistelrooy will look back and wonder why he went to ground so easily when presented with a clear chance to score, ex-Red Mark Wilson will look back and wonder how a penalty wasn't awarded against him when clearly handling the ball in full view of referee Barber, and fans will look back and wonder just what might have been if we'd taken a clean sheet into the half-time break. Looking back, though, will not give us any points. **SB**

THE TEAMS

BARTHEZ ⑧

FERDINAND ⑧   BROWN ⑦

O'SHEA ⑧   SILVESTRE ⑧

VERON ⑨   KEANE ⑦
BECKHAM ⑧   SCHOLES ⑦

FORLAN ⑦   SOLSKJAER ⑦

MORRISON
LAZARIDIS   DEVLIN
KIROVSKI
SAVAGE
CISSE
SADLER   KENNA
M JOHNSON   CUNNINGHAM
VAESEN

United Subs Giggs ⑦ for Keane (85), Richardson ⑥ for Scholes (73), P Neville ⑦ for Solskjaer (75)
Birmingham Subs Horsfield for Lazaridis (51), Powell for Cunningham (63), Woodhouse for Sadler (68)

MATCH STATS

MANCHESTER UNITED		BIRMINGHAM CITY
62%	POSSESSION	38%
6	SHOTS ON TARGET	2
14	SHOTS OFF TARGET	4
13	CORNERS	4
13	FOULS CONCEDED	11
1	BOOKINGS	2
0	RED CARDS	0

United star man ⭐

Seba Veron Touches of genius

Manchester United
FORLAN (37), BECKHAM (73)
Birmingham City

2
0

SAT 28 DECEMBER 02 ◆ 3PM ◆ OLD TRAFFORD ◆ ATT: 67,640 ◆ FA PREMIERSHIP ◆ REF: M DEAN ◆ ENTERTAINMENT: ●●●●○

Two goalscorers united

Seba summons the spirit of Cantona

THIS WAS A GAME WHERE THE SCORELINE DEFINITELY DID NOT TELL ALL THE STORY, AS A BATTERED BIRMINGHAM FOUND THEMSELVES ON THE SHARP END OF A QUITE BRILLIANT UNITED ATTACKING DISPLAY.

ON ANOTHER DAY IT COULD HAVE been many more for United, yet such was our profligacy that it took two fine Fabien Barthez saves to earn us the deserved three points. It was that kind of day. However, we were treated to a display from Seba Veron that had you wishing that the ref wouldn't blow the final whistle. It was perhaps the greatest individual performance – and I don't say this lightly – at Old Trafford since the delightful days of Cantona.

Seba has had his critics, and not just from those in the media (who always take such delight when a big transfer at United doesn't immediately come off) as United supporters have also seemed split on the subject. The pleasing aspect is that he has never hidden during his United career, admitting that he has underperformed and promising not only to see out his contract but to prove the doubters wrong. We can only hope that this is now the real start of a beautiful relationship.

Fergie, as ever, has stuck up for his player and that loyalty really began to reap its rewards in December as Veron started to seek the ball, lead the play and, crucially, see his visionary passes come off. I can't even adequately describe one cross with the outside of his 'other' boot, let alone perform it myself, but it was undoubtedly the highlight of a magnificent performance.

You began to lose count of how many chances we created, yet failed to put away. The ball bobbled around the box (for Scholes especially), went just wide or, as Fergie commented later, we lingered with the ball and tried to walk it in the net when a early shot would have made more of an impact.

But these are minor criticisms far outweighed by the positives. Both Ferdinand and O'Shea swept forward, enabling our strikers to drift into open space. Diego, the butt of many an ABU joke during the autumn, has started scoring goals that win us points too. And in goal two Barthez saves could even be described as Schmeichel-esque.

As Steve Bruce returned to familiar territory (and a warm welcome) he was reminded just how good we are at dominating home games. If Seba keeps this up we'll be doing it in some style as well. **BC**

> "We should have won by a lot more but sometimes we tried to walk the ball into the net, sometimes we were wasteful and sometimes we were unlucky"
>
> SIR ALEX FERGUSON

NEW YEAR
NEW HOPE

U NITED FANS BEGAN THE NEW YEAR buoyed by the team's revival. Post-Christmas losses at Blackburn and Middlesbrough warned against complacency, but to be tucked in second place just five points behind Arsenal was better than even the most optimistic Red could have hoped for two months before. Not only that, the team were starting to play the kind of attacking football we've come to expect over the years, and we had the exciting diversion of FA Cup and Worthington Cup ties to look forward to.

Wednesday 1 January 2003
SUNDERLAND (H)
PREMIERSHIP

Saturday 4 January
PORTSMOUTH (H)
FA CUP RD 3

Tuesday 7 January
BLACKBURN ROVERS (H)
WORTHINGTON CUP SF1

Saturday 11 January
WEST BROMWICH ALBION (A)
PREMIERSHIP

Saturday 18 January
CHELSEA (H)
PREMIERSHIP

Wednesday 22 January
BLACKBURN ROVERS (A)
WORTHINGTON CUP SF2

Sunday 26 January
WEST HAM UNITED (H)
FA CUP RD 4

Saturday 1 February
SOUTHAMPTON (A)
PREMIERSHIP

Tuesday 4 February
BIRMINGHAM CITY (A)
PREMIERSHIP

Sunday 9 February
MANCHESTER CITY (H)
PREMIERSHIP

Saturday 15 February
ARSENAL (H)
FA CUP RD 5

Manchester United
BECKHAM (81), SCHOLES (90)

Sunderland
VERON OG (5)

2
1

WEDS 1 JANUARY 03 ◆ 2PM ◆ OLD TRAFFORD ◆ ATT: 67,609 ◆ FA PREMIERSHIP ◆ REF: G POLL ◆ ENTERTAINMENT: ⬤⬤⬤⬤⬤

Scholesy goes nuts after snatching a last-gasp winner

THE TEAMS

BARTHEZ **7**

FERDINAND **8**   BROWN **8**
O'SHEA **9**   SILVESTRE **8**
     VERON **7**   KEANE **8**
BECKHAM **9**   SCHOLES **8**
   FORLAN **7**   SOLSKJAER **7**

PHILLIPS

STEWART   FLO
     KILBANE   MCCANN
MCCARTNEY   THIRLWELL   WRIGHT
         BABB   CRADDOCK
           MACHO

United Subs Carroll **7** for Barthez (29), Giggs **7** for O'Shea (63), G Neville **6** for Veron (89)
Sunderland Subs Williams for McCann (14), Proctor for Flo (72), Oster for Stewart (84)

MATCH STATS

MANCHESTER UNITED		SUNDERLAND
61%	POSSESSION	39%
14	SHOTS ON TARGET	1
17	SHOTS OFF TARGET	3
10	CORNERS	2
12	FOULS CONCEDED	14
2	BOOKINGS	1
0	RED CARDS	0

United star man ⭐

David Beckham Impresssive equaliser

Reds leave it late to sink Black Cats

> "There is not a player in the Manchester United side who cannot do something for them in attack. They have such drive and determination"
>
> HOWARD WILKINSON

THERE'S A NICE SYMMETRY TO THIS – MY FIRST UNITED MATCH REPORT, 20 YEARS ALMOST TO THE DAY SINCE MY DAD FIRST TOOK ME TO OLD TRAFFORD WHERE, AS AN EIGHT YEAR OLD, I WATCHED BIG RON'S REDS DRAG OUT A DRAW WITH SUNDERLAND...

THINGS GOT OFF TO A BAD START, with Barthez flailing a mis-hit punch at a Thirlwell free-kick which fell to Gavin McCann. His speculative lob went goalward and Seba Veron fluffed a miscontrolled header back over Rio Ferdinand and into the net. Woeful stuff, although in mitigation, the off-balance Argentine should have had a shout from the waiting Ferdinand to leave the ball to him.

From then on, someone ought to have issued Sunderland with a flood warning, as United flowed forward relentlessly, pummelling Macho's goal with an incredible 31 attempts in all. So, to convert only two chances might sound profligate, and on

another day, United might have strolled away with a bagload, but take nothing away from Sunderland's performance: they held their shape (a desperate, defensive 9-0-1 formation) and failed to sink under the red tide. They might be wretched going forward, but they defended manfully against a relentless onslaught, and were within a whisker of pulling off a shock result. It was impressive, if frustrating, viewing, but United never panicked, just kept attacking with style and composure on a slippy, scuffed surface, in a manner that harked back to the rapid, ferocious free-flowing football of the late 90s.

O'Shea played a blinder at right-

back, and there were also several good performances: Beckham, who topped off a good game with a lovely equaliser after a one-on-one with the Sunderland keeper. Needless to say, the skipper was everywhere: passing, mopping up, keeping possession, all the time urging the Reds on and on. Also impressive was Silvestre and it was his determination that set up the winner at the start of stoppage time, with his cross being nutted almost through the netting by the charging Scholes arriving in the six-yard box at just the right moment.

The roof nearly came off the ground, as 60-odd thousand relieved Reds inside Old Trafford cheered their heads off.

On the way out of the stadium, we saw a taxi with the logo 'New United' on the windscreen. No, same old United, leaving it to the last minute to send us home happy. Long may it continue. **MS**

THE TEAMS

CARROLL ⑤
FERDINAND ⑥   BLANC ⑥
G NEVILLE ⑦   SILVESTRE ⑥
        P NEVILLE ⑦   KEANE ⑦
BECKHAM ⑧   RICHARDSON ⑥
        GIGGS ⑤
        VAN NISTELROOY ⑦

MERSON   TODOROV
QUASHIE   STONE
        DIABATE
TAYLOR   HARPER
    TAVLARIDIS   FOXE   PRIMUS
            HISLOP

United Subs Stewart ⑤ for Keane (45), Scholes ⑥ for Richardson (59), Brown ⑥ for Silvestre (81)
Portsmouth Subs Pericard for Merson (45), Burton for Stone (86)

MATCH STATS

MANCHESTER UNITED		PORTSMOUTH
54%	POSSESSION	46%
10	SHOTS ON TARGET	3
6	SHOTS OFF TARGET	4
13	CORNERS	2
7	FOULS CONCEDED	17
0	BOOKINGS	2
0	RED CARDS	0

United star man ★

David Beckham Top performance and a bendy free-kick

Manchester United
VAN NISTELROOY 2 (5 PEN, 81 PEN), BECKHAM (17), SCHOLES (90)

Portsmouth
STONE (39)

4
1

SAT 4 JANUARY 03 ◆ 12.30PM ◆ OLD TRAFFORD ◆ ATT: 67,222 ◆ FA CUP 3RD ROUND ◆ REF: M RILEY ◆ ENTERTAINMENT: ❂❂❂❂○

Group hug for our goalscoring trio

Oh, for a little of that Cup magic

> "When I came to England people said to watch how different the cup matches are, and they are. They are great games to play in"
>
> RUUD VAN NISTELROOY

I'M SICK OF CUP HOME GAMES. IT MAY BE A CHURLISH STATEMENT, AND I'M SURE FANS OF SAY, EVERTON, DARLINGTON AND CITY WOULD GLADLY SWAP PLACES WITH ME, BUT THESE MATCHES ARE SO PREDICTABLE.

THE OPPOSITION FANS ARRIVE IN their thousands, armed with balloons, tickertape and stupid-looking jester hats, then proceed to accuse our support of the following: a) not singing; b) not being from Manchester; c) having the referee on our side; and d) being 'glory hunters'. Clubs must be giving out instructions on 'How to behave at Manchester United away' with the tickets.

The night before the game against Portsmouth I'd been out in Manchester for a few drinks with some friends. When asked by a Blue mate if I was looking forward to the next day's game, I explained I wasn't, making the following predictions of what would happen:

"Pompey fans will arrive at Old Trafford and proceed to shoot their mouths off to fanzine sellers on Sir Matt Busby Way, with comments like, 'I've not heard a Manc accent yet,' or 'You must be as tired as us, having made the early morning trip all the way from Cornwall?' They will then get into the ground and sing about us being '60,000 muppets'. Then they will dispute every free-kick/throw-in/corner given United's way and chant 'You've only got 12 men' at the final whistle. On the pitch, United will score, then Portsmouth will get one and United will up a gear for 10 minutes to kill the game off."

The day after the match, I call my City mate and remind him of my prediction but with a few of the gaps filled in: "Ruud scored a penalty, Becks was brilliant throughout and bent in an amazing free-kick. Then Portsmouth scored and rallied for a while before another Ruud penalty and a Scholes chip won it for us. 4–1".

The point I was making was that in recent years we've enjoyed very few new cup experiences. I'd love to have watched United away at Scunthorpe, like Leeds did. In fact, any away draw against a non-Premiership side would have made a nice change. Of late, apart from Burnley away in the Worthington Cup, we've been starved of new and different cup experiences.

Oh well, at least having secured the victory we've got the next round to look forward to. Er, scratch that last bit, we've got West Ham at home. Typical. **PD**

Manchester United SCHOLES (58)
Blackburn Rovers THOMPSON (61)

1
1

TUE 7 JAN 03 ◆ 8PM ◆ OLD TRAFFORD ◆ ATT: 62,7401 ◆ WC SEMI-FINAL (1ST LEG) ◆ REF: U RENNIE ◆ ENTERTAINMENT: ⬤⬤⬤⬤⬤

Scholesy gives United the lead

THE TEAMS

BARTHEZ ①

FERDINAND ⑥ BROWN ⑦

G NEVILLE ⑦   SILVESTRE ⑦

P NEVILLE ⑤   VERON ⑥

BECKHAM ⑦   SCHOLES ⑦   GIGGS ⑤

VAN NISTELROOY ⑥

YORKE   COLE

THOMPSON   TUGAY   FLITCROFT   DUNN

NEILL ▯   TAYLOR   TODD   MCEVELEY ▯

FRIEDEL

United Subs Solskjaer ⑦ for Giggs (74),
Forlan ⑥ for P Neville (82)
Blackburn Subs Gillespie for Dunn (19),
Jansen for Thompson (66)

MATCH STATS

MANCHESTER UNITED		BLACKBURN ROVERS
54%	POSSESSION	46%
4	SHOTS ON TARGET	3
6	SHOTS OFF TARGET	3
13	CORNERS	4
17	FOULS CONCEDED	12
1	BOOKINGS	2
0	RED CARDS	0

United star man

Paul Scholes Another confident display

Is there a Cup game going on?

> **"It was a funny atmosphere. It didn't seem like the semi-final of the Cup to me. It never really got going"**
>
> SIR ALEX FERGUSON

NERVES, URGENCY, PASSION, DESIRE…
WE'VE EXPERIENCED ENOUGH SEMIS IN
RECENT YEARS TO BE ABLE TO LIST THE
USUAL INGREDIENTS. UNFORTUNATELY, IT
SEEMS THAT OLD HABITS DIE HARD WHEN
IT COMES TO THE WORTHINGTON CUP.

IT MAY NO LONGER BE A GLORIFIED reserve game, but with 5,000 empty seats and an atmosphere like a pre-season friendly (albeit slightly on the chillier side), it certainly didn't feel like the penultimate step on the road to a "major" trophy.

The latter stages of the League Cup are almost alien to us nowadays, and it seems they're also alien to the players. The lacklustre form of the Christmas period returned with passes going astray, attacks regularly breaking down and the opposition being allowed too much time and space to dictate the midfield.

Maybe the Football League had anticipated the lack of enthusiasm and provided the one ingredient in football guaranteed to liven up any affair – in Uriah Rennie they introduced the only man on earth capable of making enemies in an empty room and he stamped his authority on the game with his usual mix of strange decisions and strutting which, even in this lacklustre environment, was enough to raise the most placid supporter's temperature. Mr Rennie, however, was not the only factor that sent United fans home shaking their heads. This match was a stark reminder that the problems of a few months ago have not simply evaporated into thin air. The struggle to break down defences,

the lack of quality in the final ball and sometimes even the absence of urgency still lingers, as, unfortunately, does the ability to self-destruct.

This could have been a tale of a result ground out: an uninspiring performance somehow ending in a 1–0 win thanks to Scholes' goal. However, as we have seen time and again, one lapse of concentration is all it takes, and this time it allowed David Thompson to sneak in the away goal Rovers deserved.

Blackburn went for the win despite having the home leg to come. It fuels the worry of many United fans that Old Trafford is no longer the fortress it once was when a side can play two strikers, three attacking midfielders and have the confidence to bring a third striker on at 1–1.

Still, a draw is a draw. Sir Alex has never lost a domestic semi final. Now is the time, then, to remember what such games are all about. **AM**

THE TEAMS

HOULT

SIGURDSSON   MOORE   GILCHRIST

A CHAMBERS   CLEMENT

KOUMAS   JOHNSON   WALLWORK

DICHIO   ROBERTS

VAN NISTELROOY 7

SOLSKJAER 7   SCHOLES 7   BECKHAM 8

P NEVILLE 7   KEANE 8

SILVESTRE 7   G NEVILLE 7

BROWN 7   FERDINAND 5

BARTHEZ 6

WBA Subs Dobie for Sigurdsson (75), Balis for Chambers (86) **United Subs** Forlan 5 for Solskjaer (67), O'Shea 6 for Keane (81)

MATCH STATS

WEST BROMWICH ALBION		MANCHESTER UNITED
53%	POSSESSION	47%
2	SHOTS ON TARGET	6
7	SHOTS OFF TARGET	6
2	CORNERS	6
12	FOULS CONCEDED	9
0	BOOKINGS	1
0	RED CARDS	0

United star man ⭐

Roy Keane The beating Red heart of the team

West Bromwich Albion 1
KOUMAS (6)

Manchester United 3
VAN NISTELROOY (8), SCHOLES (22), SOLSKJAER (55)

SAT 11 JANUARY 03 ◆ 3PM ◆ THE HAWTHORNS ◆ ATT: 27,129 ◆ FA PREMIERSHIP ◆ REF: N BARRY ◆ ENTERTAINMENT: ✪✪✪✪✪

Game over: Ole's 55th minute strike put the result beyond doubt

Reds cruise victory at the Hawthorns

AFTER THE EARLY SCARE OF JASON KOUMAS' SIXTH-MINUTE STRIKE, IT TOOK UNITED A FULL 22 SECONDS FROM THE RESTART TO RESTORE PARITY.

IF THE REST OF THE MATCH WAS anything to go by, it was a surprise it took that long.

Having Keano back is much like having a new heart: the rest of the body might all be in good working order, but without a strong heartbeat, it just can't function properly. Roy Keane is the heart and soul of Manchester United, and God forbid we lose him for good. For two seasons now he's had long lay-offs, and like last year, when we only just missed out, his recent return to the side saw us trailing the Gunners again. Let's just hope those few points won't be oh-so-crucial this time.

With that in mind, this game at West Brom was a must-win fixture. After two shocking defeats over Christmas, it was essential that our away form improved, and though West Bromwich Albion cannot provide much of a benchmark of our form, the hour that United actually played was more than enough to give assurance to the travelling hordes that there's still much to fight for in terms of Premiership success this season. Around the 60 minute mark, and with 'job well done' stamped indelibly on the fixture, United players moved back down the gears to conserve energy. Nobody watching minded, least of all the home support. They'd had a torrid time watching their heroes torn apart and, for a while at least, they could compete for a bit of pride.

> "Sometimes these games are harder than those against the top teams because they are in a relegation fight. They gave their all but it just wasn't enough on the day"
>
> ROY KEANE

At the final whistle, the Manchester United fans assembled to cruelly rib the Albion supporters about their almost certain return to the Nationwide League. The police presence in the United end (the first time I've ever witnessed police in riot gear and with shields in a domestic fixture ever) did nothing but smile, for the threat of trouble, a bit of 'afters' from the home fixture, never materialised. What did become apparent, however, was the quality of the United support, a factor that has been consistently picked up by the players at games away from Old Trafford this season. Ryan Giggs songs (despite his absence), constant encouragement, old classics and, of course, the usual teasing of whoever the match is against — it's just a pity those at Old Trafford who don't have anything positive to say couldn't be there to witness it. **SB**

Manchester United SCHOLES (39), FORLAN (90)

Chelsea GUDJOHNSEN (30)

2

1

SAT 18 JAN 03 ◆ 12.30PM ◆ OLD TRAFFORD ◆ ATT: 67,606 ◆ FA PREMIERSHIP ◆ REF: P DURKIN ◆ ENTERTAINMENT: ●●●●●

THE TEAMS

BARTHEZ ⑦

FERDINAND ⑥   BROWN ⑥

G NEVILLE ⑥   SILVESTRE ⑤

P NEVILLE ⑥   KEANE ⑥

BECKHAM ⑧   SCHOLES ⑧   SOLSKJAER ⑦

VAN NISTELROOY ⑦

HASSELBAINK   GUDJOHNSEN

LE SAUX   GRONKJAER

PETIT   LAMPARD

BABAYARO   MELCHIOT

DESAILLY   GALLAS

CUDICINI

United Subs Giggs ⑥ for P Neville (45), Forlan ⑧ for Van Nistelrooy (71), Veron ⑥ for Silvestre (86)
Chelsea Subs Zola for Hasselbaink (16), De Lucas for Gronkjaer (56), Zenden for Gudjohnsen (84)

MATCH STATS

MANCHESTER UNITED		CHELSEA
52%	POSSESSION	48%
5	SHOTS ON TARGET	3
3	SHOTS OFF TARGET	5
6	CORNERS	6
10	FOULS CONCEDED	10
0	BOOKINGS	1
0	RED CARDS	0

Diego is in there somewhere...

United star man ★

David Beckham Superb crossing, again

Pretenders to the throne

> "The excitement of scoring a goal like that is Manchester United, really. Diego has been doing it all season for us and he's become a hero because of it"
>
> SIR ALEX FERGUSON

ALTHOUGH THIS WAS BILLED AS A GAME BETWEEN TITLE CONTENDERS, CHELSEA'S LACK OF CONSISTENCY IN THE LEAGUE MAKES A SUSTAINED CHALLENGE APPEAR UNLIKELY ANY TIME SOON.

NOT THAT THE BLUES AREN'T dangerous opponents. Few teams look forward to playing on the much-maligned Old Trafford pitch, but Chelsea's recent record here, along with the fact that their own ground currently resembles Southport beach, meant the West Londoners were well up for this battle for second place in the league.

However, Chelsea are symptomatic of many clubs that have got ideas above their stations since Sky came to town. They're never going to win the league, so success for them should be judged in cup runs and possibly a Champions League place. However, both club and supporters appear unable to grasp this. Just ask Gianluca Vialli, the most successful manager in the club's history, sacked for not winning the championship.

That said, his replacement Claudio Ranieri has at least got his team playing some attractive football, and it was his side who took the early initiative. Phil Neville, United's 'midfield enforcer', put Hasselbaink out the game after only 15 minutes, but this worked against the Reds as the lively Zola came on and began to pull the strings. Chelsea looked dangerous during this period, and when the impressive Petit found Gudjohnsen for a neatly finished opener after half-an-hour, it was no more than they deserved.

Doubtless, the assembled hacks were prematurely pencilling in the headlines of another Chelsea triumph in Manchester at this stage. Happily, the otherwise superb Cudicini had other ideas and just before half-time he gifted a simple clearance straight to Becks, who swiftly swung over a sumptuous cross for Paul Scholes to net for the fifth consecutive game.

It was nice to see Giggs receive a warm ovation as he entered the fray for the start of the second half, but by full-time it was Fergie's other two substitutes who had stolen the show. Veron's defence-splitting injury-time pass dropped perfectly for Forlan and his superb left foot finish sent Old Trafford into raptures, silencing the Chelsea fans mid-'mow a meadow'.

Ranieri showed refreshing realism after the game by ruling his side out of the championship race, but he may ultimately pay for this honesty as the 'title contenders' are once more condemned to 'also-rans'. **TH**

THE TEAMS

FRIEDEL

NEILL   TODD   TAYLOR   McEVELEY

FLITCROFT   TUGAY

THOMPSON   DUFF

YORKE   COLE

GIGGS ⑥   VAN NISTELROOY ⑤

SCHOLES ⑥

VERON ⑧   BECKHAM ⑦

KEANE ⑧

SILVESTRE ⑥   G NEVILLE ⑦

BROWN ⑦   FERDINAND ⑥

BARTHEZ ⑥

Blackburn Rovers Subs Gillespie for Duff (34)
United Subs Butt ⑥ for Scholes (79), Forlan ⑥ for Van Nistelrooy (84)

MATCH STATS

BLACKBURN ROVERS		MANCHESTER UNITED
45%	POSSESSION	55%
4	SHOTS ON TARGET	10
3	SHOTS OFF TARGET	3
6	CORNERS	6
11	FOULS CONCEDED	15
2	BOOKINGS	0
0	RED CARDS	0

United star man ★

Paul Scholes He scores goals... match-winning goals

Blackburn Rovers COLE (12) **1**
Manchester United SCHOLES 2 (30, 42), VAN NISTELROOY (77 PEN) **3**

WED 22 JANUARY 03 ◆ 8PM ◆ EWOOD PARK ◆ ATT: 29,048 ◆ LEAGUE CUP SF 2ND LEG ◆ REF: J WINTER ◆ ENTERTAINMENT ◆◆◆◆

Cardiff, here we come!

Bring on the Scousers!

JUST BEFORE CHRISTMAS, 7,000 UNITED FANS BUOYED UP BY THE TEAM'S RESURGENT FORM TRAVELLED TO EWOOD PARK ONLY TO WITNESS A FLAT, DISAPPOINTING UNITED PERFORMANCE.

BARELY A MONTH LATER, A SIMILAR number made the trek again, despite Blackburn's impressive first leg performance threatening to make this another joyless trip for the Red Army.

Happily, that wasn't to be the case, but the eventual ease of our victory belied the quality and hard work that went into achieving it. It's easy to forget now, but at 1–0 down with Cole bearing down on Barthez's goal, it seemed as if United's four-year wait

for a Cup final appearance would be extended still further. But Barthez parried Cole's shot and United began to assert their superiority.

Our eventual ascendancy can be attributed in part to some fine tactics from Fergie's coaching staff, employing a system where United's middle four operated more centrally than usual: bunching tight and stifling Rovers' creativity.

Although Blackburn had enjoyed midfield dominance in our previous visit to Ewood Park, this time Keane and co earned the right to play before Paul Scholes stepped up to drag United back into the tie. His first goal came from a Beckham centre which bounced kindly off his chest allowing him time to slot home. 12 minutes later, he scored his second after a classic United counter-attack. Keane broke up a Blackburn move then worked the ball to Neville, who marauded down the right before supplying the killer

> "I can't complain. We have played a really good team tonight. There is no disgrace in losing to a side of that quality"
>
> GRAEME SOUNESS

cross for the in-form Salfordian to sidefoot the ball past Friedel.

The second half saw chances for both sides, notably an Andy Cole miss with the score at 2–1, and Brad Friedel was again in fine form. But he could do nothing about Ruud's 77th minute penalty after he'd upended the Dutchman in the box.

As United supporters screamed "Bring on the Scousers", the Football League and Worthingtons were no doubt rubbing their hands at the prospect of such a heavyweight final contest for the tournament. However, some Reds are seriously considering, in the event of victory in Cardiff, that the trophy be donated to Manchester City, given our traditional indifference towards the competition and our neighbours' lack of acquaintance with silverware. Anyway, as Sir Alex pointed out recently, when Liverpool are the opposition you don't need a cup for motivation. **JPO**

Manchester United
GIGGS 2 (8, 29), VAN NISTELROOY 2 (49, 58),
P NEVILLE (50), SOLSKJAER (69)

6

West Ham United

0

SUN 26 JANUARY 03 ◆ 1PM ◆ OLD TRAFFORD ◆ ATT: 67,181 ◆ FA CUP 4TH ROUND ◆ REF: S BENNETT ◆ ENTERTAINMENT: ⊙⊙⊙⊙⊙

Rio invites the ref to join the happy Red throng

THE TEAMS

BARTHEZ **7**
FERDINAND **7** O'SHEA **7**
G NEVILLE **7** P NEVILLE **7**
VERON **8**
BECKHAM **7** KEANE **7**
SCHOLES **7**
VAN NISTELROOY **9** GIGGS **8**

DEFOE
SINCLAIR COLE BOWYER
CARRICK CISSE LOMAS
MINTO
PEARCE BREEN
JAMES

United Subs Forlan **7** for Scholes (45),
Butt **7** for Veron (51), Solskjaer **7** for Beckham (63)
West Ham United Subs Dailly for Breen (79),
Johnson for Sinclair (79), Garcia for Cisse (79)

MATCH STATS

MANCHESTER UNITED		WEST HAM UNITED
59%	POSSESSION	41%
8	SHOTS ON TARGET	7
35	SHOTS OFF TARGET	2
7	CORNERS	3
5	FOULS CONCEDED	10
1	BOOKINGS	2
0	RED CARDS	0

United star man ★

Ruud van Nistelroof Masterful

We're forever scoring goals

> "West Ham are in a difficult period but you have got to give credit to our players for not allowing them any chance to improve their confidence"
>
> SIR ALEX FERGUSON

HALFWAY THROUGH THE FIRST HALF OF THIS GAME I RECEIVED A TEXT MESSAGE. JUST TWO WORDS LONG, IT SUMMED UP THE THOUGHTS OF THE MAJORITY INSIDE OLD TRAFFORD: 'LIQUID FOOTBALL'.

THE MESSAGE WAS FROM AN impressed Chelsea fan, compelled to reach for his phone after witnessing a breathtaking 27-pass move which ended with Paul Scholes striking a post. It was perhaps this moment, even more than any of the six goals, that summed up United's biggest victory since the 7–1 demolition of, ahem, West Ham three years ago.

Judging by the noise, the 9,000 confident, if not over-confident, Hammers who filled Tier Two of the East Stand were dreaming of a repeat of the game two years ago when United lost to a Paolo di Canio goal after some failed Fabien Barthez mind games.

Happily, a repeat performance was never on the cards. West Ham looked a team in crisis from the first whistle to the last: no confidence, no fighting spirit and, well, no defence. Having been made to toil for every goal recently, the wide open space for our attackers was a welcome relief and a chance to showcase the kind of football that exercises the hairs on the back of your neck.

The first half belonged to Ryan Giggs, probably not the best 45 minutes of football he's ever played, but maybe one of his most important. His two goals may go some way to resurrecting his confidence and, hopefully, his season. But he wasn't the only player to catch the eye as United ran riot. With Seba

Veron dictating play in midfield, Paul Scholes frequently escaping West Ham's weak clutches and Ruud van Nistelroy leading the line with a mix of dogged determination and fancy footwork, it wasn't surprising that every pass was soon being greeted with a shout of "Ole!" from the Old Trafford crowd.

After the break, United were awesome. Amid a West Ham collapse, three goals in the first 13 minutes eliminated any hope of a fightback; Ruud capped a great all-round performance with two goals and Phil and Ole also added one apiece to the scoresheet.

West Ham are undoubtedly a team in disarray but, all the same, two cup victories in the space of five days will boost United's confidence before a couple of potentially tricky away games at Southampton and Birmingham, when we'll be hoping for more of that liquid football. **RS**

THE TEAMS

NIEMI

TELFER · LUNDEKVAM · M SVENSSON · BENALI

OAKLEY · A SVENSSON

FERNANDES · MARSDEN

BEATTIE · TESSEM

SOLSKJAER ⑦ · VAN NISTELROOY ⑧
GIGGS ⑦
VERON ⑦ · BECKHAM ⑧
KEANE ⑦
SILVESTRE ⑦ · G NEVILLE ⑧
O'SHEA ⑧ · FERDINAND ⑨
BARTHEZ ⑦

Saints Subs Davies for Tessem (70), Jones for Niemi (86)
United Subs Carroll ⑦ for Barthez (38), Scholes ⑦ for Beckham (70), Forlan ⑦ for Van Nistelrooy (88)

MATCH STATS

SOUTHAMPTON		MANCHESTER UNITED
48%	POSSESSION	52%
2	SHOTS ON TARGET	5
9	SHOTS OFF TARGET	5
7	CORNERS	6
15	FOULS CONCEDED	14
2	BOOKINGS	0
0	RED CARDS	0

United star man ★
Rio Ferdinand Dominant in his best game yet for United

Southampton 0
Manchester United 2
VAN NISTELROOY (15), GIGGS (22)

SAT 1 FEBRUARY 03 ◆ 3PM ◆ ST MARY'S STADIUM ◆ ATT: 32,085 ◆ FA PREMIERSHIP ◆ REF: P DOWD ◆ ENTERTAINMENT: ●●●○○

Ruud's opener gave Gary some pleasure

Cracking goals and crocked goalkeepers

WE KNOW UNITED LEAVE THEIR BEST UNTIL LAST. EACH YEAR, THEY COME ALIVE FOR THE LATTER STAGES OF THE SEASON AND SO FAR 2003 IS PROVING TO BE NO EXCEPTION TO THE RULE.

NEW YEAR HAS SEEN A WELCOME return to the swagger of old, culminating in a clinical, destructive FA Cup win over West Ham the week before. With the Birmingham fixture moved, the team and the fans had a rare week off ahead of the long trip down South, but it didn't affect that momentum.

Right from the whistle, the Reds were off and running. Exploding out of the blocks to nullify any home advantage, the team took the game by the scruff of the neck, dictating play against a side that has been very powerful at home this season. When Giggsy's twice-attempted shot made it 2–0 only 22 minutes in, the Saints didn't know what had hit them.

Maybe the returning habit of winning aways has quickly spread on to the terraces or perhaps it's the fact that this was a rare, and much appreciated, second consecutive Premiership away fixture kicking off at the unfamiliar time of 3pm on a Saturday. Whatever the reason, this game (along with the game at West Brom) was as good a day out and as good an atmosphere as I can remember in our recent travels. On the website forums and message boards of ABU teams across the country, our unique and boisterous travelling support is finally getting the praise it deserves.

The team winning, the fans supporting – it's all very contagious. The brilliant team spirit is best

> "It's just a bad kick for our goalie Antti Niemi. He's in better nick than Fabien Barthez though – he was sitting in my office smoking fags in the second half!"
>
> GORDON STRACHAN

summed up by the group hug after every goal scored of late. Today, Gary Neville looked like he was about to decapitate Ruud, such was his joy after the Dutchman's crucial opening goal.

Elsewhere, Rio had his best game in a United shirt and we kept a rare but deserved clean sheet despite the loss of Fabien Barthez through injury on 38 minutes. Some home fans took the opportunity to cheer his departure on a stretcher, but when an unfortunate coincidence also saw their keeper Antti Niemi carried off in the second half the United fans gave him a sympathetic round of applause.

Never mind that: Arsenal's injury-time equaliser at home to Fulham meant they maintained their lead at the top; United did what they had to do, and in some style too. The players and fans are ready for the season run-in. The chase is on. **BC**

Birmingham City 0
Manchester United 1 VAN NISTELROOY (56)

TUE 4 FEBRUARY 03 ◆ 7.45PM ◆ ST ANDREWS ◆ ATT: 29,475 ◆ FA PREMIERSHIP ◆ REF: S DUNN ◆ ENTERTAINMENT: ●●●●●

All you need is gloves

THE TEAMS

VAESEN
CUNNINGHAM   UPSON
KENNA   CLEMENCE   CLAPHAM
D JOHNSON   DUGARRY   SAVAGE
MORRISON   JOHN

GIGGS ⑦   VAN NISTELROOY ⑦
VERON ⑦   SCHOLES ⑦   BECKHAM ⑦
KEANE ⑧
SILVESTRE ⑦   G NEVILLE ⑦
BROWN ⑦   FERDINAND ⑦
CARROLL ⑥

Birmingham City Subs Lazaridis for John (63), Kirovski for Morrison (78), Devlin for Kenna (84)
United Subs Solskjaer ⑤ for Van Nistelrooy (82)

MATCH STATS

BIRMINGHAM CITY		MANCHESTER UNITED
46%	POSSESSION	54%
1	SHOTS ON TARGET	3
3	SHOTS OFF TARGET	10
3	CORNERS	5
10	FOULS CONCEDED	16
1	BOOKINGS	1
0	RED CARDS	0

United star man ★

Roy Keane His grit was the perfect foil for Seba's flair

Cold comfort at humdrum Brum

> "Sir Alex will go up the M6 with a glass of red wine and three points. We are bitterly disappointed we did not nick something"
>
> STEVE BRUCE

I WAS IN MY CAR DRIVING TO OLD TRAFFORD TO CATCH THE COACH TO BIRMINGHAM WHEN I SUDDENLY REALISED THAT I'D LEFT MY GLOVES ON MY BED. DESPITE BEING TIGHT FOR TIME, I TURNED THE CAR AROUND AND DROVE BACK HOME TO GET THEM. IT WAS AN INSPIRED DECISION.

I'VE NEVER BEEN TO ST. ANDREWS before so I was very much looking forward to this fixture. I kind of knew what to expect, a Man city-supporting mate having warned me of a hot reception and a big fence around the away end. Those Blues know their stuff about lower division clubs, but then that's because they've so often supported one themselves!

On this occasion the Brummies were subdued, although the relatively poor atmosphere in the ground could be put down to the bitter weather; I'd say the home fans were too cold to be vociferous.

By the second half, everyone around me was complaining about the Arctic temperatures. In between singing the new Seba Veron version of *Take Me Home United Road*, that is. For the record it goes like this: "Came from Rome to Old Trafford, Juan Sebastian Veron. He's a genius, from Argentina. Juan Sebastian Veron." The first line could be better but I still think it's a great song for a truly great player. Which is exactly what he has become for us, a great player who is now making a telling contribution every week.

Anyway, in between renditions, I noticed that people were looking at me enviously. Or rather at my mittens. I noticed less clapping than usual during songs but I think the booming noise that my gloves made every time I applauded helped keep the volume levels up.

I was at my noisiest when Ruud van Nistelrooy swivelled on a Silvestre pass to shoot low into the net despite being surrounded by defenders. He's class, that Dutchman. And sensible too, judging by the fine pair of gloves he was wearing!

I apologise that this match report has become so preoccupied with my hand-warmers, but I genuinely did appreciate my gloves during this game. Having seen the error of their ways, my mates will now be following my example for the forthcoming fixtures. Which means that not only am I wise when it comes to matchday attire, but I'm now a trendsetter too. Bonus. **PD**

THE TEAMS

CARROLL ⑤
FERDINAND ⑥   BROWN ⑥
G NEVILLE ⑤   BROWN ⑥   SILVESTRE ⑥
KEANE ⑦
BECKHAM ⑤   SCHOLES ⑤   VERON ⑥
VAN NISTELROOY ⑥   GIGGS ⑤

FOWLER   ANELKA
BERKOVIC
JENSEN   HORLOCK   FOE   SUN JIHAI
DISTIN   HOWEY   SOMMEIL
NASH

United Subs Butt ④ for Veron (77), Solskjaer ⑤ for Giggs (89)
City Subs Wright-Philips for Horlock (66), Goater for Fowler (85), Benarbia for Berkovic (85)

MATCH STATS

MANCHESTER UNITED		MANCHESTER CITY
56%	POSSESSION	44%
4	SHOTS ON TARGET	4
7	SHOTS OFF TARGET	3
10	CORNERS	4
11	FOULS CONCEDED	13
1	BOOKINGS	1
0	RED CARDS	0

United star man ★
Roy Keane Could have been worse if it wasn't for him

Manchester United 1
VAN NISTELROOY (18)

Manchester City 1
GOATER (84)

SUN 9 FEB 03 ◆ 12.30PM ◆ OLD TRAFFORD ◆ ATTENDANCE: 67,646 ◆ FA PREMIERSHIP ◆ REF: A WILEY ◆ ENTERTAINMENT: ●●●○○

The hardest 'Spot The Ball' competition ever?

More derby day disappointment

ALL TALK BEFORE THE GAME WAS OF REVENGE FOR THE DEFEAT SUFFERED AT THE LAST EVER MAINE ROAD DERBY IN NOVEMBER.

MUCH HAS BEEN SAID OF SIR ALEX Ferguson's reaction to that result, and the players had made all the right noises in the press leading up to the match. The game gave those with wounded egos a chance to atone for the disgracefully lacklustre performance that day.

Meanwhile, we supporters hoped the return fixture would provide an opportunity to put November's defeat to bed and throw that result back at City supporters. Predictably, those fans disgraced themselves yet again, spewing out obscenities throughout the pre-match airing of 'The Flowers of Manchester', played as a tribute to those who lost their lives in Munich tragedy 45 years ago this week.

The stage appeared to be set for a performance of verve and passion, and in this context United's display was baffling. Having scored after 18 minutes through Ruud Van Nistelrooy and controlled the first half, Manchester United were well-placed to inflict a heavy defeat on our rivals. But, following a wasted opportunity from Van Nistelrooy when put through by David Beckham on 56 minutes, United sat back and lethargically let the Blues come back into the game.

But for our ever-dependable captain Roy Keane, City could easily have won this match. Shaun Goater and Ali Benarbia were brought into the fray as Kevin Keegan's side had gradually passed their way into the

match, and the two subs combined for Goater's headed equaliser. But for Nicolas Anelka's handball in stoppage time, Goater may well have grabbed a winner for the 'laser blues'. Such a result was unthinkable at half-time, but the United side again proved to be their own worst enemy by not killing the game off when they had the chance.

The lack of commitment at times would suggest they have learnt little from the game at Maine Road three months ago.

As supporters, we have nothing but praise for the attitude the team has shown to fight back from the November derby day debacle – particularly gutsy displays against Arsenal and Liverpool in the league. But we must wonder if the players really understand how much this fixture means to us Reds after they under-performed for the third successive derby. **TH**

> "I thought I had more time to score but the player came and robbed me. It was an important moment in the match"
> RUUD VAN NISTELROOY

Manchester United 0
Arsenal EDU (34), WILTORD (52) 2

SAT 15 FEBRUARY 03 ◆ 12.15PM ◆ OLD TRAFFORD ◆ ATT: 67,209 ◆ FA CUP ROUND 5 ◆ REF: J WINTER ◆ ENTERTAINMENT: ●●●○○

Sometimes there are no words...

See you at Highbury...

IT WAS SUPPOSED TO BE THE BATTLE OF BRITAIN. NORTH v SOUTH. FERGUSON v WENGER. KEANO v VIEIRA. BUT FOLLOWING THE HYPE – AND IN STARK CONTRAST TO THE LAST TIME WE MET ARSENAL IN THE FA CUP – THE MATCH WILL BE REMEMBERED AS RYAN GIGGS v THE EMPTY NET.

WE MAY AS WELL GET IT OUT OF the way now. For ours and Giggsy's sake. Just as Ryan's wonder goal in 1999 will be played time and again, you'll all be unfortunate enough to catch this miss on TV repeatedly over the remainder of the season. Although it was just one of those things that happens every now and

UNITED FAILED TO TEST VISITING GOALKEEPER DAVID SEAMAN WITH A SINGLE SHOT ON TARGET 0

then, it didn't stop many Manchester United fans in the ground slumping to their seats in response. They immediately knew it was going to prove the defining moment of the game.

United had set about the opening 10 minutes as if they had followed the pre-match build-up about this encounter being the competition's decider. But the response from the team following the miss that we all wanted wasn't forthcoming. The players' heads seemed to sink and though Gary Neville tried to gee up his teammates (including a consoling pat on the back for Giggsy himself), Arsenal's opening goal seemed inevitable. It came as a result of an unjustly awarded free-kick and Edu's subsequent strike took a wicked deflection off David Beckham's shoulder to rub salt into an already blistering wound.

... and sometimes everyone has something to say

The game was the total antithesis of our league win over Arsenal last December. Perhaps that is why, as the Gunners celebrated at the end like they had won the Cup itself, this debilitating result should be put into context. First pathos, then perspective. You win some and, unfortunately, every once in a while you lose some.

Each tackle won late on seemed to produce a reaction from the Arsenal player involved as if they had just been run over by an invisible herd of stampeding elephants. For a side that had played such high-tempo football, they really didn't need to resort to such undignified tactics.

Ryan Giggs will bounce back from this. United will. We all will. Old Trafford emptied in despair. Just a bad day at the office, to be compounded in the following days with tabloid front and back pages about what did and did not happen in the dressing room after the game.

Just like the match itself, let's forget about that, follow Fergie's advice and move on. **BC**

> "We were unlucky because Ryan had done the hardest thing in getting round the keeper and the defender, but couldn't finish it. At 2–0 down it was always going to be difficult"
>
> SIR ALEX FERGUSON

CHAPTER FIVE

JUVE BEEN WARNED!

CHAMPIONS LEAGUE FOOTBALL was back on the agenda after a two-month winter break. Unbeaten in the Premiership since the turn of the year, United would face their sternest test in Europe so far this season, taking on Juventus twice in one week. And having disposed of the United Old Boys (aka Blackburn) in the Worthington Cup semi-final, Ferguson's in-form side were strong favourites to turn over Liverpool in the final at the Millennium Stadium a few days later. But things don't always go to plan...

Wednesday 19 February
JUVENTUS (H)
CHAMPIONS LEAGUE PHASE TWO

Saturday 22 February
BOLTON WANDERERS (A)
PREMIERSHIP

Tuesday 25 February
JUVENTUS (A)
CHAMPIONS LEAGUE PHASE TWO

Sunday 2 March
LIVERPOOL,
WORTHINGTON CUP FINAL

Wednesday 5 March
LEEDS UNITED (H)
PREMIERSHIP

Wednesday 12 March
FC BASEL (H)
CHAMPIONS LEAGUE PHASE TWO

Saturday 15 March
ASTON VILLA (A)
PREMIERSHIP

Tuesday 18 March
DEPORTIVO (A)
CHAMPIONS LEAGUE PHASE TWO

Saturday 22 March
FULHAM (H)
PREMIERSHIP

Manchester United BROWN (3), VAN NISTELROOY (85)

Juventus NEDVED (90)

2
1

WED 19 FEB '03 ◆ 7.45PM ◆ OLD TRAFFORD ◆ ATT: 66,703 ◆ CL PHASE 2 ◆ REF: K NIELSEN ◆ ENTERTAINMENT: ⭘⭘⭘⭘⭘

This is how it feels to score your first goal for United

THE TEAMS

BARTHEZ **7**

FERDINAND **7**   BROWN **8**

G NEVILLE **7**   KEANE **7**   BUTT **7**   SILVESTRE **7**

SCHOLES **6**

BECKHAM **7**   GIGGS **7**

VAN NISTELROOY **7**

ZALAYETA   TREZEGUET

NEDVED

TACCHINARDI   CAMORANESI

DAVIDS

ZENONI   PESSOTTO

MONTERO   FERRARA

CHIMENTI

United Subs O'Shea **8** for Silvestre (52), Solskjaer **7** for Scholes (80), Forlan **6** for Giggs (90) **Juventus Subs** Olivera for Trezeguet (65)

MATCH STATS

MANCHESTER UNITED		JUVENTUS
47%	POSSESSION	53%
2	SHOTS ON TARGET	3
3	SHOTS OFF TARGET	8
3	CORNERS	7
9	FOULS CONCEDED	16
2	BOOKINGS	2
0	RED CARDS	0

United star man ⭐

Wes Brown Unlikely first scorer!

Putting the boot into flu-ventus

> "There has been a lot written and said about David Beckham this week but he is always there for us, for the crowd and for everybody at this club. I have a great respect for him for that"
>
> RUUD VAN NISTELROOY

THERE WAS NO SHORTAGE OF BUILD-UP TO THIS GAME, WITH THE PAPERS JAMMED FULL OF REPORTS ABOUT SIR ALEX OF GOVAN'S ATTEMPT TO KNIGHT BECKS USING A SIZE NINE INSTEAD OF A SWORD.

THERE WAS ALSO TURMOIL IN THE opposition camp where, thanks to a bout of flu, Juventus had been robbed of five of their players, including Buffon and Thuram.

Despite early probing from Juventus, United struck first – David Beckham's right-sided free-kick landing plum on Wes Brown's head for a third-minute goal.

The Juve fans didn't go under as their team went a goal down, singing and reacting to every incident.

And at least they don't just sing "Shall we sing a song for you?" or "Shhhhh!"

On the pitch, there was also plenty going on. There's still no finer sight than an up-for-it Ryan Giggs at full tilt, running at the opposition like "a dog chasing a piece of silver paper in the wind," as Fergie once drooled. However, watching our hip-strung captain pacing around the centre circle was a sad sight. Roy was uncharacteristically caught in possession or gave the ball away on occasions, and Davids often had the beating of him.

In the second half, referee Kim Milton Nielsen was at his dummy-headed worst when he ignored a clear penalty and red card incident after Chimenti pulled down Van Nistelrooy. Play was waved on, Scholes whacked the loose ball against the post, and that was that. Ruud got some satisfaction

in the end though, dinking a perfect Beckham cross over Chimenti to secure his 21st (21st!) European goal for the club.

This wasn't a particularly fluid United performance. Attempts at overwhelming Juve petered out or broke against the Italians' solid backline. United looked urgent at times, dominating the game but then subsiding into an introverted, slightly lax style of play. It was all a little dispirited.

Juventus had chances, with Zalayeta constantly harassing our back four. Nedved was influential in Del Piero's absence and scored late on when he put a curving, hopeful 30-yard pass past Barthez.

Happily, the goal did not influence the final result as United opened up a five-point lead at the top of Group D. Three games left, a quarter-final place looks a near-cert. Boot-iful. **MS**

THE TEAMS

JAASKELAINEN

N'GOTTY LAVILLE BERGSSON

MENDY CHARLTON

IVAN CAMPO

OKOCHA GARDNER

DJORKAEFF

PEDERSEN

SOLSKJAER ⑥ VAN NISTELROOY ⑤

GIGGS ④ BECKHAM ⑤

VERON ④ KEANE ⑤

O'SHEA ⑤ G NEVILLE ⑤

BROWN ⑥ FERDINAND ⑤

BARTHEZ ⑦

Bolton Subs Salva for Pedersen (58), Barness for Mendy (82), Nolan for Djorkaeff (85)
United Subs Forlan ⑤ for Giggs (58), P Neville ⑤ for Brown (74), Butt ⑤ for Veron (80)

MATCH STATS

BOLTON WANDERERS		MANCHESTER UNITED
40%	POSSESSION	60%
5	SHOTS ON TARGET	2
8	SHOTS OFF TARGET	4
8	CORNERS	5
14	FOULS CONCEDED	11
1	BOOKINGS	1
0	RED CARDS	0

United star man ★

Fabien Barthez Saved lacklustre United from defeat

Bolton Wanderers 1
N'GOTTY (61)

Manchester United 1
SOLSKJAER (90)

SAT 22 FEBRUARY 03 ◆ 12PM ◆ REEBOK STADIUM ◆ ATT: 27,409 ◆ FA PREMIERSHIP ◆ REF: ANDY D'URSO ◆ ENTERTAINMENT: ●●○○○

Becks' cross lead to United's last-gasp equaliser

A bad day at the office

ASK ANY CRITIC YOU LIKE FOR THE REASONS BEHIND MANCHESTER UNITED'S COMPLETE DOMINANCE OF THE ENGLISH GAME IN RECENT YEARS AND THERE WILL BE ONE CONSTANT THEME.

DESPITE THE SKILL AND CLASS OF the players, they worked and battled as hard as a team fighting relegation.

This was the ethic that set United apart. As fans we took pride in our team's drive, spirit, passion, workrate and belief. Whether they played Bolton or Bayern Munich, the effort and commitment was identical.

The one question on the lips of the 3,000 Reds leaving the Reebok Stadium on Saturday afternoon was, where have these trademark qualities gone? And more importantly, how

do we go about getting them back?

So far this season, United have dropped 29 points in the league. Incredibly, 24 of those have been dropped against clubs in the lower half of the Premiership. Although this means we're having more success against our rivals, dropping points like confetti against teams at the wrong end of the table is uncharacteristic of the Manchester United we know and love.

Just before the Liverpool game this season, Carlos Quieroz stated that he didn't think United should get involved in a battle, simply play their football. Worryingly, it seems that in this desire to play football we have forgotten how to stand toe-to-toe with teams like Bolton and outfight them, before using superior class to beat them.

This was just another episode of an all too familiar story this season where a team outfought, unsettled

> "We didn't give Beckham a sniff all game but he has the quality to punish you if you give him time and space and that's what we did"
>
> SAM ALLARDYCE

and simply wanted a result more than a United side looking bereft of ideas and, at times, passion.

Bolton played well, deserving their breakthrough in the second half after being unlucky not to be ahead at half-time. The lack of reaction from United spoke volumes. Only one real chance was created before Ole Gunnar Solskjaer salvaged some pride, if not the whole season, with what might prove to be a crucial last-minute equaliser.

But the goal provided little comfort for Reds heading home and theories were flying as to why those United trademarks had gone. Such words may be harsh and emotive, but we are the fans, we're passionate, we want to win, and we feel every single result. We simply expect those representing us on the pitch to do the same. Just like they used to. **RS**

Juventus | 0
Manchester United | 3
GIGGS 2 (15, 41), VAN NISTELROOY (60)

WED 25 FEBRUARY 03 ◆ 7.45 ◆ STADIO DELLE ALPI ◆ ATT: 59,111 ◆ CHAMPIONS LEAGUE ◆ REF: M MERK (GER) ◆ ENTERTAINMENT: ✪✪✪✪✪

2–0: Giggs finishes off a wonderful individual goal

Ver-on form Reds destroy Juve on their own turf

YOU PROBABLY ONLY GET TWO OR THREE OF THESE A SEASON: RESULTS THAT REMIND YOU EXACTLY WHAT MAKES OUR CLUB SO SPECIAL. YOU FEAR THE WORST, EXPECT LITTLE AND COME AWAY OVERFLOWING WITH PRIDE HAVING SEEN YOUR TEAM SHINE. THAT'S HOW IT WAS IN TURIN.

> JUVENTUS HAD 14 SHOTS, FIVE MORE THAN UNITED, BUT MANAGED JUST TWO STRIKES ON TARGET
>
> **2**

SITTING IN A BAR OUTSIDE THE Stadio Delle Alpi before the match I couldn't find anyone predicting a victory. Well, I did find one but he was so drunk that I'm not sure he'd have even found the ground.

Opinion among the less inebriated was that Juventus would punish us for our recent sloppy play and probably hammer us if the Bolton Wanderers display was repeated. Optimism was in short supply.

15 minutes into the game, a minute after Juve had seen an effort come back off the post, things changed. Veron's persistence saw him rob Zambrotta of the ball on the edge of their penalty area before playing in Ryan Giggs who calmly slotted past Buffon. The 4,000 United fans jumped around

deliriously, dodging countless missiles launched from the home sections as they did so.

Juventus probed for an equaliser but Giggs produced one of those pieces of magic that only he and a handful of others in the world game can. Picking the ball up in his own half he danced past two Juve defenders before rolling the ball right-footed into Buffon's net. Delirium ensued in the away end once again. More objects rained down on us but the Juve fans' aim was decidedly worse than Giggs' and

Nights like this don't come along very often

THE TEAMS

BUFFON

FERRARA   MONTERO

THURAM

CONTE   DAVIDS   ZAMBROTTA

CAMORANESI   NEDVED   DI VAIO

TREZEGUET

FORLAN ⑤   SOLSKJAER ⑦

VERON ⑨   BECKHAM ⑧

BUTT ⑧   P NEVILLE ⑧

O 'SHEA ⑧   G NEVILLE ⑧

KEANE ⑨   FERDINAND ⑧

BARTHEZ ⑦

Juventus Subs Tudor fior Conte (45),
Salas for Di Vaio (45), Pessotto for Zambrotta (66)
United Subs Giggs ⑨ for Forlan (8), Van Nistelrooy ⑦
for Giggs (48), Pugh ⑦ for O'Shea (60)

MATCH STATS

JUVENTUS		MANCHESTER UNITED
55%	POSSESSION	45%
2	SHOTS ON TARGET	6
12	SHOTS OFF TARGET	3
7	CORNERS	2
16	FOULS CONCEDED	16
1	BOOKINGS	1
0	RED CARDS	0

United star man ⭐

Seba Veron The passmaster's best display for United

SHOTS	1
PASSES	71
PASS COMPLETION %	82%
TACKLES	5
ASSISTS	1
DRIBBLES	8
FOULS	1

What the papers said...

"The proud Juventus
institution was turned into
record-book fodder by
Manchester United. With a
win that exploited the
accident-prone Italian
champions, they have
become the first side to
reach the Champions
League quarter-final for
a seventh consecutive year.'
Kevin McCarra, The Guardian

'Ryan Giggs showed last night why Inter Milan are
desperate to buy him – and why United would be
bonkers to sell him. Giggs scored a wonder goal and
was the star of a magnificent United display in
which they swatted aside the Italian League
leaders.The win ensured Alex Ferguson's men
qualified for the Champions League quarter-finals
for the seventh successive season, a record for the
competition. Rumours of their demise have clearly
been exaggerated.'
Shaun Custis, The Sun

joyous celebrations continued.

English fans are not welcomed to the Delle Alpi. References to the Heysel disaster in 1985 adorned banners and when a large placard with the words 'English Animal' was unveiled there was no mistaking their loathing. Their insult was directed straight back at them on the hour mark.

"Three nil to the animals!" chanted the United fans having seen Ruud Van Nistelrooy score his 22nd Champions League goal in only his 23rd match in the competition.

"Arrivederci," sang United fans as Italians flooded out.

Ryan Giggs would rightly be given the plaudits in the next day's papers but it was Roy Keane and Seba Veron who received most praise by Reds post-match. The skipper's performance at centre-half made a mockery of his recent criticism, while everyone agreed it had been Veron's best display in a Red shirt. He'd been awesome.

Nights like this don't come along often and this one will live long in the memory. **PD**

> "They were world class. They can create all sorts of problems from lots of different situations. They have great quality and you need to be able to move quickly to counter them. We weren't able to do that"
>
> MARCELLO LIPPI, JUVENTUS COACH

Liverpool GERRARD (39), OWEN (86)

Manchester United

2
0

SUN 2 MARCH 03 ◆ 2PM ◆ MILLENNIUM STADIUM ◆ ATT: 74,500 ◆ LEAGUE CUP FINAL ◆ REF : P DURKIN ◆ ENTERTAINMENT: ⊙⊙⊙⊙⊙

The stage was set for a United victory, but Liverpool keeper Dudek was in unbeatable form

Bored into submission

WHETHER THE AIR CONDITIONING WAS TURNED UP A LITTLE FROM OUR LAST VISIT THERE (SADLY ANOTHER DEFEAT TO LIVERPOOL) IS UNCLEAR, BUT THE TEMPERATURE UNDER THE ROOF WAS DEFINITELY A LOT COOLER THAN LAST TIME.

AND DESPITE THE FACT WE WERE playing in a 'major' final against historically our most bitter rivals, it never warmed up.

The Millennium Stadium, Cardiff, is a magnificent venue, of that there is no doubt, and though the journey

158 UNITED MADE 158 MORE PASSES (354 TO 386) THAN LIVERPOOL

home was a nightmare due to traffic problems (compounded by the pain of defeat), justice was never done to the setting by the dour football served up from the winners.

A tactical masterstroke it may have been, but boring United into a comatose state serves no football fan, least of all your own. While we may suffer defeats at the hands of Arsenal, at least we do so in the knowledge that they are a magnificent footballing side. Being beaten by 'Wimberpool' is harder to swallow.

While half-time came and went

with us a goal behind, thanks to a hugely deflected Steven Gerrard shot, the non-descript nature of the first 45 minutes was replaced by an almost relentless Manchester United assault on the Liverpool goal in the second period.

But whereas our league victory at Anfield was helped in no small measure by the dodgy goalkeeping of Jerzy Dudek, this game was decided in Liverpool's favour by the recently re-instated 'keeper. The Pole made save after save with whatever part of his body he managed to get

Seba rides an attempted tackle from Diouf

THE TEAMS

DUDEK

HENCHOZ ■ HYYPIA

CARRAGHER   RIISE

DIOUF   GERRARD   HAMANN   MURPHY

HESKEY   OWEN

VAN NISTELROOY ⑦

SCHOLES ⑥

GIGGS ⑥   BECKHAM ⑥

VERON ⑧   KEANE ⑦

SILVESTRE ⑤   G NEVILLE ⑦

BROWN ⑥   FERDINAND ⑥

BARTHEZ ⑦

Liverpool Subs Baros for Heskey (61),
Smicer for Baros (89), Biscan for Diouf (89)
United Subs Solskjaer ⑥ for Brown (74)

MATCH STATS

LIVERPOOL		MANCHESTER UNITED
49%	POSSESSION	51%
7	SHOTS ON TARGET	9
1	SHOTS OFF TARGET	3
3	CORNERS	4
11	FOULS CONCEDED	19
1	BOOKINGS	0
0	RED CARDS	0

RUUD v DUDEK

STATS	RUUD	STATS	DUDEK
GOALS	0	GOALS LET IN	0
ON TARGET	3	CLEAN SHEET	1
OFF TARGET	2	SAVES	8
PASSES	21	SAVES / SHOTS	100%
PASS %	67%	CATCHES	0
FOULS	1	PASSES	31
OFFSIDES	1	PASS %	48%

United star man

Seba Veron Lead United's second-half assault

---

in the way of strikes from Ruud Van Nistelrooy and co.

With Seba Veron outstanding and Roy Keane seemingly nearer to full fitness, it appeared only a matter of time before a breakthrough. It never came though. Ryan Giggs, David Beckham, Paul Scholes and Mikale Silvestre were out of sorts and we were reminded again of the need for a striker to compliment Ruud, a problem which I'm sure will be resolved soon.

But, if you asked any United fan before the game which result

mattered more – this trophy or three points in the following midweek game against Leeds United, they'd almost all say the latter.

The common media consensus that this game offered our most realistic chance of silverware this season is debatable considering our fine showing in Turin. What isn't open to debate however, is the fact that I'd rather not win a thing than play the 'football' that Liverpool are currently doing.

The beautiful game? Not for Liverpool it isn't. **SB**

> "We expected Liverpool to play the way they did but we were far too slow in our build-up and when we went behind we didn't improve on that"
>
> SIR ALEX FERGUSON

What the papers said...

'This was a deeply damaging day for such a proud club, a day which may be remembered as the moment when they went out of two competitions in the space of four hours. Defeat here was compounded by Arsenal having extended their Premiership lead to eight points by vanquishing Charlton. United may have to concentrate on the league – the Champions League.'
Henry Winter, The Daily Telegraph, 3 Mar 2003

'Roy Keane says United are plotting a hazardous course aiming for Europe as their silverware salvation. The Reds' domestic double cup quest has been wrecked because, as their Worthington Cup ambition collapsed in Cardiff, the Premiership title was slipping from their sights across the M4 in London. But Old Trafford captain Keane says United can still land a trophy to appease the letdown fans.'
Stuart Mathieson, Manchester Evening News

Manchester United RADEBE OG (20), SILVESTRE (79) 2
Leeds United VIDUKA (64) 1

WED 5 MARCH 03 ◆ 8PM ◆ OLD TRAFFORD ◆ ATT: 67,135 ◆ FA PREMIERSHIP ◆ REF: G POLL ◆ ENTERTAINMENT: ●●●○○

Oh Mickey, you're so fine!

It's the result that counts

WITH ARSENAL EIGHT POINTS CLEAR AT THE HEAD OF THE
PREMIERSHIP AND THE MOOD AMONG REDS DOWNBEAT
AFTER THE WORTHINGTON CUP FINAL DEFEAT, VICTORY
AGAINST LEEDS WAS IMPERATIVE.

FOLLOWING A LUMBERING performance in Cardiff, Sir Alex implemented changes with Gary Neville and Ryan Giggs relegated to the bench, the latter just eight days after he earned the headline "Fantastico Giggs" in *La Gazzetta Dello Sport* for his heroics in Turin.

Leeds United have endured issues of their own this season and when one fan demanded the resignation of Peter Ridsdale, his directors, Terry Venables and Brian Kidd on a pre-match radio phone-in, it illustrated that all is not well in the people's republic of stubborn.

United started brightly, as they have often done this season, and a 20th-minute own goal from Radebe rewarded our early dominance

against a Leeds team missing six regulars and unrecognisable from the side that last visited Old Trafford. The goal came after David Beckham crossed for Nicky Butt before Lucas Radebe turned the ball into his own net through a crowded penalty area.

Despite chances, a second goal wasn't forthcoming and when peaceable fans weren't watching evidence of the longstanding enmity between the two clubs at half-time, with a flare-up between supporters inside the ground, they wondered whether United would be ruthless

MANCHESTER UNITED BEGAN THIS MATCH EIGHT POINTS BEHIND ARSENAL IN THE TITLE RACE **8**

Young Irishman John O'Shea continues to impress

enough to kill Leeds off in the second period. They also questioned why Leeds fans were singing 'Liverpool'. Is their own team really that bad?

Aside from a wicked Alan Smith shot acrobatically saved by Barthez, Venables' side had offered little in the first half. Yet in the second period, they were much more self-assured, more purposeful. When Viduka headed an equaliser after 64 minutes, it was difficult to feel sorry for England's premier 'United'. For just as against Manchester City the

previous month, Sir Alex's players were guilty of letting poorer opposition back into the game. Luckily, with 11 minutes, Silvestre ran onto a lofted Beckham free-kick to head his first goal of the season and grab all three points.

With Keane, Veron, Silvestre and Fortune all picking up knocks, the win had come at a cost, but no matter how untidy the performance, the one thing that really mattered was eventually achieved. Victory. **AM**

> "We've picked up some knocks and injuries but we're still in the race. We need Arsenal to drop points and we need to do our job"
>
> SIR ALEX FERGUSON

Manchester United G NEVILLE (53)

Basel GIMINEZ (14)

2
1

WED 12 MAR 03 ◆ 7:45PM ◆ OLD TRAFFORD ◆ ATT: 66,870 ◆ CL PHASE 2 ◆ REFEREE: C LARSEN ◆ ENTERTAINMENT: ⊙⊙⊙⊙⊙

Gary celebrates his fourth goal in 385 games!

THE TEAMS

CARROLL ⑤

BLANC ⑤   FERDINAND ⑤

G NEVILLE ⑥   O'SHEA ⑥

P NEVILLE ⑥ ■   BUTT ⑤

FLETCHER ⑦   RICHARDSON ⑤

SOLSKJAER ⑥   FORLAN ⑤

GIMENEZ   ROSSI

CHIPPERFIELD   H YAKIN   BARBERIS

CANTALUPPI ■

ATOUBA   HAAS

M YAKIN   ZWYSSIG

ZUBERBUHLER

United Subs Giggs ⑥ for Richardson (45), Beckham ⑥ for Fletcher (73), Scholes ⑦ for Blanc (73)
Basel Subs Huggel for Rossi (63), Tum for Gimenez (77)

MATCH STATS

MANCHESTER UNITED		BASEL
53%	POSSESSION	47%
3	SHOTS ON TARGET	2
5	SHOTS OFF TARGET	10
1	CORNERS	3
18	FOULS CONCEDED	4
1	BOOKINGS	1
0	RED CARDS	0

United star man ⭐

Darren Fletcher Lively passing and slick control

Basel get brushed aside

> "I picked a side that would do us justice and no-one can point the finger at us"
>
> SIR ALEX FERGUSON

FEW REDS WILL HAVE EXPECTED MUCH FROM A GAME WHICH WAS LARGELY MEANINGLESS FROM UNITED'S PERSPECTIVE.

WITH QUALIFICATION FOR THE quarter-finals of the Champions League already secured, injuries and players being rested meant that the side Sir Alex Ferguson selected would in all probability succumb to a Basel side needing three points to have any realistic ambitions of joining their opponents in the next round. That United secured a draw masks the overwhelming disappointment at the manner of the performance felt by so many in attendance.

Ferguson was right to pick a side capable of giving Basel a game to be fair to the other two teams in the group, but the management's first concern should surely have been to the fans who pay their money to watch the game. With the result immaterial would it have been too much to expect the entertainment of those fans to take priority? United's approach in the first half was hopelessly negative and perhaps a betrayal of the attacking legacy of teams of yore. With Diego Forlan isolated up front and Phil Neville consistently lying so deep he may as well have been a fifth defender, all-out attacking football was not on Manchester United's agenda. Neither was all-out defending, however, judging from Rio Ferdinand's positioning for Basel's opener, and he took the blame for allowing the lively Giminez to smash the ball past United's second-choice keeper Roy Carroll.

Even the 1–0 deficit failed to inject any verve into United's play, the lively Darren Fletcher aside. The young Scot took advantage of his starting role, three injury-ravaged years after FA rules prevented Fergie giving him his debut at Villa Park when only 16, to impress the fans with his passing and control. If only certain other players could look to emulate his knack of knowing where to pass the ball before it's even reached him.

United improved towards the end of the half, coinciding with Ole Gunnar Solskjaer's move to centre-forward, but it wasn't until the second period that any meaningful attacks on the Swiss goal were launched. By then Ryan Giggs had replaced Richardson on the left flank but United's goal came from a less likely source. Gary Neville, courtesy of a telling deflection off Atouba, struck home only his fourth goal in 385 appearances. **MS**

THE TEAMS

POSTMA

MELLBERG   JOHNSON

SAMUEL   WRIGHT

HENDRIE   HITZLSPERGER

HADJI   BARRY

DUBLIN   VASSELL

VAN NISTELROOY 7   SOLSKJAER 7
GIGGS 7   BECKHAM 7
SCHOLES 8   BUTT 8
SILVESTRE 8   G NEVILLE 8
O'SHEA 8   FERDINAND 7
BARTHEZ 9

Aston Villa Subs Cooke for Dublin (79)

MATCH STATS

ASTON VILLA		MANCHESTER UNITED
49%	POSSESSION	51%
8	SHOTS ON TARGET	5
13	SHOTS OFF TARGET	9
6	CORNERS	6
13	FOULS CONCEDED	10
2	BOOKINGS	1
0	RED CARDS	0

United star man ⭐

Fabien Barthez Some outstanding saves repelled Villa

Aston Villa 0
Manchester United 1
BECKHAM (12)

SAT 15 MARCH 03 ◆ 12.30PM ◆ VILLA PARK ◆ ATT: 42,602 ◆ FA PREMIERSHIP ◆ REF: M DEAN ◆ ENTERTAINMENT: ⬤⬤⬤⬤⬤

Becks' early strike proved decisive

One is the magic number

> "If we can't win three- or four-nil, why not score one and make sure we don't concede? Again, Fabien was fantastic. For us he is the best goalkeeper in the world"
>
> OLE GUNNAR SOLSKJAER

IT'S A SHAME THAT RECENT HISTORY HAS DICTATED THAT MANCHESTER UNITED v ASTON VILLA IS ONE OF THE LEAST INSPIRING FIXTURES IN THE FOOTBALLING CALENDER. THAT CAN USUALLY BE EXPLAINED BY THE NEGATIVE TACTICS OF THE OPPOSITION, AND THIS GAME DID LITTLE TO BUCK THE TREND.

BUT AMONG THE UNITED FRATERNITY, both on and off the field, it was result over performance that was of the utmost importance today as we maintained our unbeaten league record of 10 games.

The result came by way of a Beckham strike at the back post, courtesy of a cross from Giggs on the left after he'd found time and space out wide. The goal followed a promising spell, during which Van Nistelrooy saw a goal disallowed, Beckham shot at the keeper from a Solskjaer cross and there was a dominance that bode well for the rest

of the game. Sadly that opening salvo was misleading as United failed to create anything of note for the remainder of the match.

Whether it's a coincidence or not, yet another early kick-off yielded another muted atmosphere and a game played out in a sonambulent manner. However, Villa did play with a greater gusto than they have in previous encounters and United old boy Dion Dublin proved a constant threat. His substitution was greeted with vast disapproval from the home crowd (a sell-out once again for a United game) and a sigh

of relief from our centre-backs. With that tactical move the game seemed all but over, as he had contributed both directly and by assist to the multitude of chances that Barthez had to save.

Although a one-goal win might not have been the game plan, as with our recent victory across the city at Birmingham, these sorts of results might be considered priceless come the end of the season.

With United content to play out time, and that drifting away slowly, Villa's last throw of the dice didn't come from anyone sent on by Graham Taylor, but instead from a male streaker whose miniscule, er, assets provided the home crowd with their biggest cheer of the day.

United fans cheered a win that was to prove even more vital later that afternoon when Blackburn's victory over Arsenal gave the title race a shake to its very foundations. **BC**

Deportivo La Coruña
VICTOR (32), LYNCH OG (47)

Manchester United

2

0

TUE 18 MARCH 03 ◆ 7.45PM ◆ EL RIAZOR ◆ ATT: 25,000 ◆ CL PHASE 2 ◆ REFEREE: V HRINAK ◆ ENTERTAINMENT: ✪✪✪✪

Young Fletcher gets stuck in

THE TEAMS

DANI MALLO

CESAR   ANDRADE

MANUEL PABLO   CAPDEVILA

VÍCTOR   ACUÑA   DUSCHER   FRAN

VALERÓN

LUQUE

GIGGS ⑤   FORLAN ⑤

BUTT ⑤   FLETCHER ⑦

NEVILLE P ⑥

PUGH ⑥   LYNCH ⑦

O'SHEA ⑥   BLANC ⑤   ROCHE ⑥

RICARDO ⑥

Deportivo Subs Scaloni for Fran (52), Djorovic for Andrade (64), Hector for Victor (77)
United Subs Stewart ⑥ for Roche (45), Webber ⑥ for Forlan (72), Richardson ⑥ for Giggs (72)

MATCH STATS

DEPORTIVO		MANCHESTER UNITED
61%	POSSESSION	39%
4	SHOTS ON TARGET	2
10	SHOTS OFF TARGET	8
7	CORNERS	1
7	FOULS CONCEDED	16
1	BOOKINGS	1
0	RED CARDS	0

United star man ★

Darren Fletcher This boy looks the part

Make way for Real Madrid!

> "I would be very happy if we were paired with Real. Facing teams like Real, Barcelona, Juventus and the rest is what the Champions League is all about"
>
> SIR ALEX FERGUSON

"WE'RE HERE IN SPAIN, YOU'RE IN MOSS SIDE." THESE WORDS RANG OUT FROM THE POCKET OF AROUND 1,000 REDS WHO'D MADE THE TRIP TO SPAIN'S 'WINDOW TO THE ATLANTIC'.

IT REMINDED US THAT, DESPITE THE irrelevance of this game, supporting a team that enables you to get a couple of days of sun, sea and sangria, all in the name of football, is something not to be taken for granted.

We're becoming familiar with the picturesque scenery of La Coruna. This was the third time we'd visited the town in 18 months. This time though, it seemed like we'd turned up on the wrong day. Less than an hour before kick-off, every bar and street was filled with Reds, their dulcet tones drifting across the Riazor's neighbouring beach, with hardly a Deportivo La Coruna fan in sight.

With important games on the horizon, Giggs was the only player

from the first XI to make the trip and Sir Alex plumped for a mixture of fringe players and youngsters.

It's always good to see the kids given a chance. The likes of Lee Roche, Mark Lynch, Michael Stewart and Danny Pugh (or Danny Pudge as he was introduced by the Spanish announcer!), all showed good temperament against more experienced players, while Darren Fletcher again showed his exciting potential on his second run-out in six days.

Of the experienced players, Blanc showed why this will be his final season as Deportivo's pacy forwards took advantage of his ageing legs. Nicky Butt, Gary Neville, Diego

Forlan and Giggs all failed to stamp their authority on the game, but one suspects they all had one eye on the fixtures ahead.

The game itself was effectively over once the unfortunate Mark Lynch had headed into his own net shortly after half-time. But thankfully the feared rout never materialised. Indeed, Lynch and the rest of the proud youngsters recovered their composure to create some good chances.

By then though the focus had shifted to the quarter-finals draw. The presence of Real Madrid as a one in three chance is worrying, and of course most teams in the last eight will be hoping to avoid them, But their qualifying form has been relatively unimpressive and as we've found out in the past, anything can happen in the knockout stages. You've got to be in it to win it. Just ask Arsene Wenger. **RS**

THE TEAMS

BARTHEZ ❼

FERDINAND ❻   BROWN ❻
G NEVILLE ❼   O'SHEA ❼

SCHOLES ❻   BUTT ❻

BECKHAM ❽   GIGGS ❻

VAN NISTELROOY ❾   SOLSKJAER ❼

SAHA   MARLET

BOA MORTE   MALBRANQUE

DJETOU   LEGWINSKI

HARLEY   KNIGHT   MELVILLE   OUADDOU

TAYLOR

No substitutions were made

MATCH STATS

MANCHESTER UNITED		FULHAM
55%	POSSESSION	45%
11	SHOTS ON TARGET	3
7	SHOTS OFF TARGET	6
9	CORNERS	5
13	FOULS CONCEDED	15
2	BOOKINGS	1
0	RED CARDS	0

United star man ★

Ruud van Nistelroop So much more than just a finisher

Manchester United
VAN NISTELROOY 3 (45 PEN, 68, 90)

Fulham

3
0

SAT 22 MARCH 03 ◆ 12.30 PM ◆ OLD TRAFFORD ◆ ATT: 67,706 ◆ FA PREMIERSHIP ◆ REF: S BENNETT ◆ ENTERTAINMENT: ⬤⬤⬤⬤⬤

2–0: Even Ruud looks shocked by his wonder goal

Triple action at Old Trafford

> "They are a much better side now – and van Nistelrooy makes a huge difference. With him I think they can beat Real Madrid and win the European Cup."
>
> JEAN TIGANA

THREE WAS VERY MUCH THE KEY NUMBER FOR THE VISIT OF FULHAM, BOTH ON AND OFF THE PITCH. ON THE OLD TRAFFORD TURF RUUD PRODUCED A STRIKING MASTERCLASS THAT SAW HIM TAKE OWNERSHIP OF THE MATCHBALL.

OFF IT, THE INDEPENDENT Manchester United Supporters Association (IMUSA) conducted a protest against the number of lunchtime kick-offs the club have had to play.

Of the 19 home fixtures that supporters buy their season tickets for, it is likely that by the end of the season only five will have been played at the traditional time of 3pm on a Saturday, and none of those since Christmas. While the lunchtime kick-offs aren't unpopular with everyone, for a large number of Manchester United supporters the fact only 10 out of 41 league and cup matches have been played at

3pm is an issue that many believe needs addressing.

To show the football authorities and the TV schedulers their discontent, IMUSA distributed 5,000 cards with the number three on them, to be held up in the crowd. Chants of "You can stick your early kick-offs up yer ****!" also made their point.

Even the players have expressed their discontent: "Who wants to eat spaghetti bolognese at 9 o'clock in the morning?" asked David Beckham recently.

However, there was little evidence of the teams' dislike for early kick-offs out on the pitch. They kept

Fulham down to half chances and when an opportunity came, from the penalty spot, United went in at half-time a goal to the good.

United's performance picked up in the second half and Ruud van Nistelrooy produced a moment to savour. Winning the ball on the half way line, he burnt off two hapless Fulham midfielders with an exceptional burst of acceleration. All the while, he had the ball perfectly under control. A neat sidestep did for the last defender then after two neat touches and a slick body swerve, he rolled the ball past Taylor to finish a sublime solo run.

In the final minute, Ruud made it three with a mis-hit but on target volley from a Ryan Giggs cross thus clinching three points for the team.

But for three truly to be the magic number the authorities should now listen to the fans, whose message was clear. **PD**

CHAPTER SIX

FINISHING
IN STYLE

THE TIME HAD COME. After months of being written off by critics, could United players complete one of the most miraculous League Championship comebacks of all-time or would all that hard work be in vain? Standing two points behind Arsenal with seven games to play and tough-looking games still to come against Liverpool, Newcastle and the defending champions, it seemed a tall order. Oh, and there was the small matter of a European Cup quarter-final against Real to take care of too...

Saturday 5 April
LIVERPOOL (H)
PREMIERSHIP

Tuesday 8 April
REAL MADRID (A)
CHAMPIONS LEAGUE QF 1

Saturday 12 April
NEWCASTLE UNITED (A)
PREMIERSHIP

Wednesday 16 April
ARSENAL (A)
PREMIERSHIP

Saturday 19 April
BLACKBURN ROVERS (H)
PREMIERSHIP

Wednesday 23 April
REAL MADRID (H)
CHAMPIONS LEAGUE QF2

Sunday 27 April
TOTTENHAM HOTSPUR (A)
PREMIERSHIP

Saturday 3 May
CHARLTON ATHLETIC (H)
PREMIERSHIP

Sunday 11 May
EVERTON (A)
PREMIERSHIP

Manchester United
VAN NISTELROOY 2 (PEN 5, PEN 65), GIGGS (78), SOLSKJAER (90)

4

Liverpool

0

SAT 5 APRIL 03 ◆ 12.30AM ◆ OLD TRAFFORD ◆ ATT: 67,639 ◆ FA PREMIERSHIP ◆ REFEREE: M RILEY ◆ ENTERTAINMENT: ◉◉◉◉○

Easy! Ryan makes it three

That's United 4 (four), Liverpool 0

BEFORE THE GAME I FEARED THE WORST. HOW COULD I DO ANYTHING BUT? WITH SIX DEFEATS TO OUR ARCH ENEMIES IN THE LAST SEVEN CLASHES, SEVERAL REDS WERE BEGINNING TO THINK THAT AT BEST THEY HAD A CURSE ON US, AT WORST THEIR DOMINATION WAS DUE TO SUPERIOR TACTICS.

BUT THERE WAS HOPE. IN OUR defeats, Liverpool have seemingly been able to dictate the pace of the game and strike on the break. But at Anfield our victory was born of grit and determination, of keeping the tempo high, and of attacking relentlessly. As the whistle blew for the beginning of this game, and our

players immediately tore savagely into our Merseyside foes, we knew we'd be alright.

Four minutes gone and a deserved penalty put us a goal in front. Should Hyypia have been sent off? On countless Saturdays, up and down the country, an equal number of refs show red as show yellow for

such tackles. But being down to 10 men did little to alter Liverpool's approach anyway. Their attacking intentions are habitually non-existent, so there was no reason to make changes.

Any doubts that United might play for a draw were now firmly out of mind. Mikael Silvestre was unlucky to have his goal wiped off when Mike Riley determined there had been a foul on Dudek, but it was impossible to see from whom. Though the scoreline read only 1–0 at half-time, the game was over as

640
UNITED HAD 640 TOUCHES OF THE BALL, 199 MORE THAN LIVERPOOL

4–0: Ole finds a gap between Traore's legs and inside the near post to complete the rout

long as United continued to dictate the play. Soon after the break, Scholes was felled in the box when running onto a pass. Ruud popped up to dispatch the penalty, killing any lingering hopes from the travelling Scousers that they might nick a point.

At this point Liverpool became the only team ever to play for a draw while being two goals down. But United were having none of it, and with confidence high two more successful strikes from Ryan Giggs and Ole Solskjaer saw the scoreline

take a more realistic look. What's more, our Premiership hopes began to look slightly less far fetched. As for Liverpool's Champions League aspirations? Their chances of qualification look very slim. And if they fail to reach the top four (helped in some part by us taking all six points off them this season!) then we can rest easy over the summer in the knowledge that Houllier will have no money to strengthen their inadequate squad. How great is football! **SB**

> "It hurts. I have to admit that. It hurts the players, the staff and the fans"
>
> GERARD HOULLIER

Real Madrid · FIGO (12), RAUL 2 (28, 49) · **3**
Manchester United · VAN NISTELROOY (52) · **1**

TUE 8 APRIL 03 ◆ 7.45PM ◆ SANTIAGO BERNABEU ◆ ATT: 75,000 ◆ CL QUARTER-FINAL 1ST LEG ◆ REF: A FRISK ◆ ENTERTAINMENT: ✪✪✪✪✪

Could this away goal prove vital?

Reds take a Bernabeu battering

IT SHOULD ALL HAVE BEEN ABOUT EUROPE'S TWO BIGGEST CLUBS GOING HEAD-TO-HEAD, A SPECTACLE OF EXHILARATING FOOTBALL. INSTEAD, FOR MANY OF UNITED'S 4,000-STRONG FOLLOWING IT WAS ABOUT BEING CRACKED ACROSS THE HEAD BY POLICE TRUNCHEONS.

REAL MADRID COMPLETED 85% OF THEIR PASSES IN THIS SPELLBINDING DISPLAY OF FOOTBALL 85

THE MOOD IN AND AROUND THE centre of Madrid had been good all day. As usual, there were squares filled with Manchester United fans drinking and breaking into the occasional song, but only if this kind of behaviour can be construed as 'hooliganism' were the Spanish press right in their portrayal of the invading English.

Entering the ground an hour before the game it was obvious that the system the police had put in place for supporters entering the ground was a recipe for disaster. With United fans' penchant for arriving late (we're spoilt by the easy access at Old Trafford), I knew there was going to be trouble. I was right. Watching the mayhem below I witnessed hundreds of United fans pushing to get in, anxious that they might miss kick-off. There were still 45 minutes to go before the start at this point but already the situation was chaotic.

United fans at the front were pushed forward by those behind. The police then baton-charged them backwards. Men, women and children were hit. The joy with which some of the Spanish police struck out was sickening to see.

Beckham battles with Makalele

MATCH STATS

REAL MADRID		MANCHESTER UNITED
53%	POSSESSION	47%
7	SHOTS ON TARGET	7
10	SHOTS OFF TARGET	6
4	CORNERS	4
12	FOULS CONCEDED	20
0	BOOKINGS	4
0	RED CARDS	0

RAUL	HEAD TO HEAD	RUUD
90	MINUTES	90
2	GOALS	1
2	SHOTS ON TARGET	4
1	SHOTS OFF TARGET	3
53	PASSES	24
81%	PASS COMPLETION %	83%
6	DRIBBLES	12
0	FOULS	3

United star man

Ruud van Nistelrooy One of the few to show his true form

What the papers said...

"Sir Alex Ferguson will have needed an oxygen mask last night. The Manchester United boss ridiculously claimed on the eve of this blockbuster that Real Madrid do not have a team to make you catch your breath. Well, his side were left gasping for air as they were taken apart by Madrid's superstar cast. Raul, Luis Figo, Zinedine Zidane and Ronaldo left United's Champions League chances in tatters."
Danny Fullbrook, Daily Star

"This was fantasy football without budget restrictions, a dazzling demonstration of why there was never any need to resort to the kind of tactics Manchester United's manager spoke of on the eve of this match. In the Bernabeu, Del Bosque's side were magnificent, all but ending this quarter final as a contest with three wonderful goals from Luis Figo and Raul (2) in the first 48 minutes."
Matt Lawton, Daily Mail

These unsavoury incidents completely tainted the atmosphere of what should have been a great European away day. Long after kick-off fans were still coming in clearly shaken, others injured and the vast majority very angry.

And the game? Well, it merely worsened the mood among the visiting hordes. I can't help feeling that the United players contributed to their own downfall. The defending for a start could have been better, with a number of players appearing to show too much respect to Real and allowing them far too much space. Still, Zidane, Raul and Figo were superb and the rest of their team very good.

At 3–0 down, United fans feared a rout, but Ruud van Nistelrooy's header gave us a chance and really the Reds should have added to that goal. Sadly, they weren't able to score and the second leg sees us with an uphill struggle to progress to the semi-finals of the Champions League for the second year in succession. But we haven't given up hope just yet. **PD**

> "It is a massive challenge but the away goal gives us a ray of hope. It will be very difficult but if we score first it could be an interesting night"
>
> SIR ALEX FERGUSON

Newcastle United
JENAS (21), AMEOBI (89)

2

Manchester United
SOLSKJAER (33), SCHOLES 3 (34, 38, 52), GIGGS (44), VAN NISTELROOY (PEN 58)

6

SAT 12 APRIL 03 ◆ 12.30PM ◆ ST JAMES' PARK ◆ ATT: 52,164 ◆ FA PREMIERSHIP ◆ REF: S DUNN ◆ ENTERTAINMENT: ✪✪✪✪✪

Ole shapes up to make it 1–1

Magpies hit for six in their own nest!

A NIGHT OUT IN NEWCASTLE, OR NEWCASTLE GATESHEAD AS THE TOURIST LITERATURE NOW CALLS IT, IS NOT FOR THE TIMID. LARGE GROUPS OF SCANTLY-ATTIRED YOUNG FEMALES ROAM THE STREETS FROM PUB TO PUB, THE SHRILL OF THEIR VOICES FILLING THE GEORGIAN SPLENDOUR OF GREY STREET.

AS USUAL, THERE WAS AN AIR OF alcopop-fuelled confidence in the toon the night before the game. Pubs advertised 'United' v 'Man Utd' on fluorescent boards, and pundits in the local evening newspaper were unanimous in their predictions for the big game: Newcastle to win. No doubt.

BEFORE THIS MATCH, PAUL SCHOLES HAD GONE 16 GAMES WITHOUT A GOAL FOR CLUB OR COUNTRY
16

The following day, a Keiron Dyer exclusive in *The Sun* added to the mood of optimism as the young star outlined his plans not only to put one over Man United but also to oust Paul Scholes from the England team. Oh dear.

When the gifted Jeenas (and Jermaine would like it known that

it's Jee-nas as opposed to Jen-ass) hit a belting shot which swerved past Barthez after 20 minutes, a bright day started brilliantly for all but 3,000 inside St James' Park.

But United (that's the one which has a need for a trophy cabinet) were level 12 minutes later when a clever Giggs cross enabled Solskjaer to beat the offside trap and score. And a second went in two minutes later. Giggs was again the provider, Scholes the finisher. 2–1.

Incredibly, United scored again to make it three in six minutes. Giggs

Hat-trick hero Scholes may keep his England place for a while yet (sorry, Keiran)

THE TEAMS

GIVEN

WOODGATE   BRAMBLE

HUGHES   JENAS   DYER   BERNARD

SOLANO   BELLAMY   SHEARER ■   ROBERT

VAN NISTELROOY (6)

SCHOLES (9)

GIGGS (8)   KEANE (6)   BUTT (6)   SOLSKJAER (7)

O'SHEA (5)   SILVESTRE (7)   FERDINAND (7)   BROWN (7)

BARTHEZ (6)

Newcastle Subs Viana for Robert (15),
Lua Lua for Solano (66), Ameobi for Viana (66)
United Subs Forlan (6) for Giggs (45),
G Neville (6) for O'Shea (49), Blanc (6) for Brown (66)

MATCH STATS

NEWCASTLE UNITED		MANCHESTER UNITED
52%	POSSESSION	48%
7	SHOTS ON TARGET	11
8	SHOTS OFF TARGET	4
6	CORNERS	6
8	FOULS CONCEDED	9
1	BOOKINGS	0
0	RED CARDS	0

DYER	HEAD TO HEAD	SCHOLES
90	MINUTES	90
0	GOALS	3
0	SHOTS ON TARGET	4
2	SHOTS OFF TARGET	1
68	PASSES	49
90%	PASS COMPLETION %	80%
7	DRIBBLES	4
0	FOULS	1

United star man

Paul Scholes Put Newcastle's young guns in their place

What the papers said...

'Manchester United took a fearful mauling in Europe in midweek but remain the Real Madrid of their own backyard. At least it looked that way against Newcastle United, who began the week with theoretical title ambitions of their own and ended it with a meek surrender that ensures the issue will now be decided at Highbury on Wednesday."
Paul Wilson, The Observer

'It was as though Manchester United had returned from Spain infected with the bug of beautiful football – as though they had stolen the Madrid manual and spent three days cramming. For Zidane, Luis Figo, Roberto Carlos and Raul read Paul Scholes, Giggs, John O'Shea and Ruud van Nistelrooy. This was the most gobsmacking transformation since Leslie Ash had her lips done."
Andy Dunn, The People

(who else?) played a ball to Brown who knocked it back for Scholes who fired a bullet shot past Given.

"Shearer, what's the score?" sang happy Reds, their anger at Alan's early transgressions against half the United team now subsided. A minute before the break, O'Shea beat Hughes with a drag-back and hit a shot that smashed off the bar. Giggs netted the rebound to make it 4–1, triggering chants of "Shearer for Sunderland".

The rout continued after the break. Mr Dyer saw Scholes seal his hat-trick on 51 minutes when he converted a Gary Neville cross. A sixth followed seven minutes later – Bramble bringing down Diego for a penalty which Ruud converted.

To their credit the Newcastle fans, whose team had only conceded 10 goals in 16 previous home games, got behind their lads despite United fans' cruel chants of: "Who put the ball in the Geordies' net? Half of Man United". Ameobi's late goal was some reward, but it did little to take the shine off a truly excellent Manchester United display. **AM**

> "On Tuesday I saw United outsmarted by Madrid. Today I've seen them outskill us and kill us off with their movement"
>
> SIR BOBBY ROBSON

Arsenal HENRY 2 (51, 62)

Manchester United VAN NISTELROOY (24), GIGGS (63)

2

2

WED 16 APRIL 03 ◆ 8PM ◆ HIGHBURY ◆ ATTENDANCE: 38,164 ◆ FA PREMIERSHIP ◆ REFEREE: M HALSEY ◆ ENTERTAINMENT: ●●●●●

Ruud lifts the ball over Taylor to make it 1–0

Arsenal get a dose of the blues

THE BIGGEST GAME OF THE SEASON IS JUST MINUTES AWAY, AND YET GARY NEVILLE AND DAVID BECKHAM ARE LINING UP WITH THE SUBSTITUTES AND FABIEN BARTHEZ IS PARTAKING IN A SPOT OF SHOOTING PRACTICE.

HAS THE SUN GOT TO ME? WAS being squashed on the tube with a load of sweaty Gooners getting here the final straw in a season of high tension? I had to wonder, but on reflection pre-match events pretty much summed up our season.

Fabien gave one of his worst

CLINICAL MANCHESTER UNITED SCORED WITH OUR ONLY TWO SHOTS ON TARGET IN THIS MATCH **2**

displays in a Red shirt at this ground last time around, but his season to date has been relatively free of the errors that plagued him last term. The sight of Gary and David on the bench was also significant. These are not players who have been dropped for poor performances. They have just been forced out by the brilliance of others (step forward John O'Shea and Ole Solskjaer).

And United's performance was typical of a team oozing confidence. We attacked from the off and were

unlucky not to score inside the first 15 minutes – Scholes and Van Nistelrooy both wasting chances they'd usually do better with.

When the goals finally came, it was United piling on the style – the first a great run and chip by Ruud, the second a great cross by Ole and header by Giggsy – and Arsenal relying on the luck – their first deflecting off Henry's calf, the second counting despite being a mile (at least) offside.

The result leaves everything still to play for, but it would take a

Get in there! Giggsy's goal earned the point

Nailbiting stuff: Becks looks on from the bench

> "As a team we were fantastic. We worked very hard to get a result here"
>
> RUUD VAN NISTELROOY

brave man (very brave if you're that bloke who's just wagered £110,000!) to bet against United now. That it was Arsene Wenger complaining about the officials and not Sir Alex at the final whistle spoke volumes. The linesman's error had cost us a goal and two points, whereas Sol Campbell's red card late on had counted for little in this game. Could it be the Frenchman is preparing his excuses early? If United keep playing like this he'll be needing every one of them. **SS**

Manchester United VAN NISTELROOY (20), SCHOLES 2 (41, 60)   **3**
Blackburn Rovers BERG (24)   **1**

SAT 19 APRIL 03 ◆ 3PM ◆ OLD TRAFFORD ◆ ATT: 67,626 ◆ FA PREMIERSHIP ◆ REF: A D'URSO ◆ ENTERTAINMENT: ●●●●○

Ricardo reprieves himself for felling Andy Cole with a fine penalty save from Dunn

Scholes at the Double!

A MONTH AGO FERGIE ANNOUNCED THE ONSET OF "SQUEAKY BUM TIME". SUCH A STRANGE PRONOUNCEMENT WAS MET WITH BEMUSEMENT IN SOME QUARTERS BUT FOR THOSE WHO'VE BEEN THROUGH THE EMOTIONAL MIRE WITH THIS TEAM OVER THE YEARS LITTLE EXPLANATION WAS NEEDED.

300 — UNITED'S WIN WAS THE 300TH TIME A TEAM HAS WON A PREMIERSHIP GAME 3–1

THIS SORT OF TIGHT, TENSE afternoon at the Premiership's summit was very much what the manager had in mind. While many were looking at Middlesbrough as a tough test for Arsenal it was easy to overlook the difficulties a stubborn Blackburn side would present United. After all, it's a rare day a Souness side proves a pushover.

A great ball from Beckham set up Ruud to head the opener on 20 minutes. Four minutes later, Rovers gained a free-kick from which 1998/99 Treble hero Henning Berg (remember that goal-line clearance in the San Siro) headed an equaliser.

Improving our goal difference relative to Arsenal's suddenly wasn't the issue, winning the game was. Similar situations in the past have seen the tension mount to unbearable levels as United have toiled with championships at stake, but with confidence surging through this side parity for Blackburn was short-lived. Phil Neville laid the groundwork following nifty footwork that delighted J-Stand before the ball fell to Paul Scholes who smashed it home to make the score 2–1.

Despite the constant danger posed

Paul Scholes, he really does score an awful lot of goals

by Damien Duff surely United could now go all out for goals. Not so. Barthez had been replaced by Ricardo during the break and his first act was to concede a penalty with a reckless challenge on Andrew Cole. However, an excellent save from Dunn's spot-kick earned the Spaniard a reprieve and with that the game was won as the belief drained from Rovers.

Paul Scholes almost notched a third straight away and he claimed it soon after following good work by Giggs and Ruud. Giggs' mediocrity

for much of the season is all the more baffling when set against his excellent displays in recent games. Today some K-Standers were heard to marvel, "He's playing like he was 17 again".

It was Giggs' persistence in robbing Cole combined with skillful footwork to play in Ruud that created the opening for the match-clinching third goal.

United could well come to rue further chances that were spurned but perhaps Lady Luck was saving a couple for Wednesday night. **JPO**

> "I am happy with the result but disappointed that we didn't score more goals"
>
> SIR ALEX FERGUSON

Manchester United
VAN NISTELROOY (43), HELGUERA (OG 52), BECKHAM 2 (71, 84)

4

Real Madrid
RONALDO 3 (12, 50, 59)

3

WED 23 APRIL 03 ◆ 7.45PM ◆ OLD TRAFFORD ◆ ATT: 66,708 ◆ CL QUARTER-FINAL 2ND LEG ◆ REF: P COLLINA ◆ ENTERTAINMENT: ✪✪✪✪✪

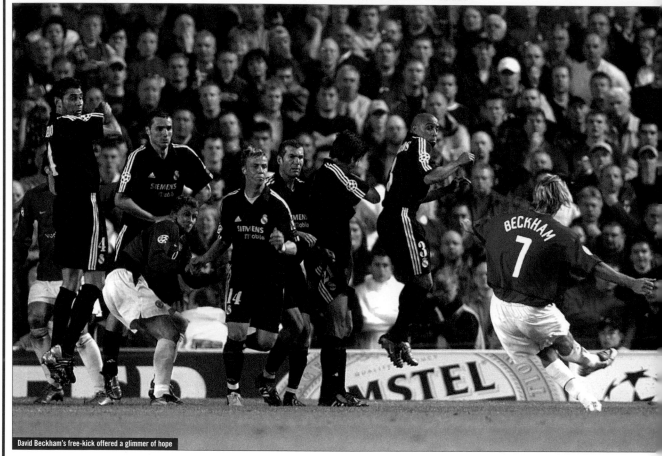

David Beckham's free-kick offered a glimmer of hope

United make a Real go of it!

RONALDO DEPARTED THE SCENE OF ONE OF THE BEST EUROPEAN CUP GAMES IN RECENT MEMORY TO A STANDING OVATION, LEAVING 66,708 PEOPLE AWE-STRUCK AT THE QUALITY THEY'D JUST WITNESSED.

AWE-STRUCK, YES. STUNNED INTO silence? Definitely not. Evidence that Old Trafford can be a cauldron of noise was here in abundance, as was the re-emerging United belief in miracles, however delusional they may seem in the cold light of day.

Starting 3–1 down against the best

3 IN A PHENOMENAL DISPLAY OF FINISHING, RONALDO SCORED A HAT-TRICK WITH HIS ONLY THREE SHOTS!

team in Europe is a tall order by anyone's standards, but Reds are conditioned to believe in the possibility of the impossible.

Unfortunately, the sinking feeling of similar nights against Dortmund, Monaco, and the last meeting with Real re-emerged after 12 minutes, as the visitors' first venture towards the Stretford End cancelled out our lifeline away goal and left United with the Spanish Himalayas to climb.

Pride, courage and the stomach for a battle were needed. Led by the outstanding Ruud van Nistelrooy,

helped out by the boundless energy of John O'Shea and boosted by the crunching tackles of Nicky Butt they showed they were in no mood to lie down, and neither were the fans.

When Ruud added yet another European goal to his tally just before the break the "maybe… just maybe" feeling was in the air once again. That hope never fully went away. Even when faced with the prospect of having to win 6-3!

David Beckham's two-goal cameo role, which arguably proved as much of a point to those in the home

It just wasn't meant to be...

THE TEAMS

BARTHEZ ⑤
FERDINAND ⑤   SILVESTRE ⑥
BROWN ⑥   O'SHEA ⑦
BUTT ⑧   KEANE ⑦
VERON ⑥ ▢
SOLSKJAER ⑦   GIGGS ⑦
VAN NISTELROOY ⑨

ZIDANE   RONALDO   FIGO ▢
GUTI
MCMANAMAN   MAKELELE
CARLOS   SALGADO
HELGUERA   HIERRO
CASILLAS

United Subs Beckham ⑧ for Veron (63), P Neville ⑥ for Silvestre (79), Fortune ⑥ for Keane (82)
Real Madrid Subs Solari for Ronaldo (67), Portillo for McManaman (69), Pavon for Figo (88)

MATCH STATS

MANCHESTER UNITED		REAL MADRID
46%	POSSESSION	54%
13	SHOTS ON TARGET	4
8	SHOTS OFF TARGET	5
3	CORNERS	1
19	FOULS CONCEDED	18
2	BOOKINGS	1
0	RED CARDS	0

United star man ★

Ruud Van Nistelrooy Pride, courage and world-class skill

MINUTES	90
GOALS	1
SHOTS ON TARGET	4
SHOTS OFF TARGET	3
PASSES	25
PASS COMPLETION %	64%
DRIBBLES	9
FOULS	2

What the papers said...

'Can there be any doubt that the 67,000 fans packed into Old Trafford and the millions watching on television witnessed one of the greatest games of all time? This was not a night for castigating United for their failure to reach the European Cup semi-finals. This was a night to revel in the brilliance of Real Madrid's hat-trick genius Ronaldo, the exquisite skills of Zinedine Zidane and the amazing recovery by Alex Ferguson's men.'
Shaun Custis, The Sun

'When Arsenal were expelled from Europe in Valencia, they slunk away. United went with their heads immeasurably higher. Whether that can still be translated into something tangible this season is of course an entirely different matter, but their chances, as always, will not be harmed by Ferguson's unbreakable defiance.'
James Lawton, The Independent

dug-out as it did to those sitting on the visitors' bench, ensured that although the war was lost, the battle was won. Although it could have all been so different had some of the numerous chances an inspired United team created had ended up the right side of the post.

The dream of appearing in an Old Trafford final is over, but our pride in the performance should live on. And if you were choosing a team fit to grace Old Trafford on 28 May, you'd surely look no further than Real Madrid. **RS**

"We showed we can match them. Winning 4-3 was a good result but it wasn't enough. Everyone gave everything they had, so we can look one another in the eye"

RUUD VAN NISTELROOY

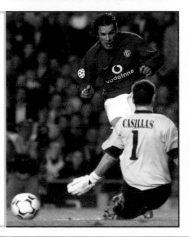

Tottenham Hotspur 0
Manchester United 2
SCHOLES (69), VAN NISTELROOY (90)

SUN 27 APRIL 03 ◆ 4.05 PM ◆ WHITE HART LANE ◆ ATT: 36,073 ◆ FA PREMIERSHIP ◆ REF: J WINTER ◆ ENTERTAINMENT:: ◉◉◉◉

Keane: back to something approaching his best

One step closer to heaven

SINCE THE WAKE-UP CALL AT MAINE ROAD LAST NOVEMBER, IT SEEMS THAT FOR MUCH OF THE SEASON WE'VE BEEN HANGING ONTO ARSENAL'S COAT TAILS WAITING, HOPING, FOR THEM TO SLIP. BUT FEW PREDICTED THEY WOULD, ESPECIALLY AFTER THE TABLOIDS HAD SO EMPHATICALLY CROWNED THEM THE 'BEST TEAM IN THE WORLD'.

OF COURSE, THE LEAGUE WASN'T settled when I wrote this report immediately after the Spurs match, but nevertheless we'd gone from hanging on coat tails to peering over shoulders. The weekend of the Tottenham game finally gave us the chance, and at a crucial stage of the season, to edge ahead and let Arsenal do the chasing for the first time. A remarkable achievement, whatever happens next.

With Bolton doing us a favour by clawing back a two-goal deficit against the Wenger boys the day before, it fell to the United players to seize the initiative that had surprisingly been handed to them.

We knew this game would be tense, and it was. We knew it would be hard-fought, and it was. However much I love these exciting finales to the season, they do the blood pressure no good at all.

Tottenham came out looking determined and despite a suggestion from the home fans that they might not be devastated by a United victory (something to do with their beloved next door neighbours, perhaps?), their team ran us hard.

UNITED WERE RELENTLESS IN ATTACK, ATTEMPTING 16 SHOTS, 11 MORE THAN THE HOME SIDE

Yes! Ruud's second goal made sure of the points

MATCH STATS

TOTTENHAM HOTSPUR		MANCHESTER UNITED
47%	POSSESSION	53%
2	SHOTS ON TARGET	8
3	SHOTS OFF TARGET	8
5	CORNERS	8
11	FOULS CONCEDED	12
0	BOOKINGS	0
0	RED CARDS	0

United star man ★

Paul Scholes A top player in top form at the right time

MINUTES	90
GOALS	1
SHOTS ON TARGET	1
SHOTS OFF TARGET	1
PASSES	61
PASS COMPLETION %	82%
TACKLES	4
FOULS	1

What the papers said...

'Manchester United are odds-on to win the Premiership title after Paul Scholes and Ruud van Nistelrooy fired them to victory over Spurs. The bookies now make Sir Alex Ferguson's men a daunting 5-1 ON to lift their eighth championship in 11 years. United held their nerve to take advantage of Arsenal bottling it in the 2-2 draw at Bolton.'
Danny Fullbrook, Daily Star

'Manchester United are winning the title race because more of their big names are showing themselves to be big men. Too many of Arsenal's marquee players are failing to impose their will in the games that really count. Spring has made United bloom. Tottenham Hotspur's neighbours — the reigning champions, remember — have gone straight to Autumn without seeing summer.'
Paul Hayward, The Daily Telegraph

Roy Carroll, in for the 'rested' Fabien Barthez, survived some early scares. Keano shrugged off the views of those who'd ludicrously suggested his glittering career had reached a dead-end at Madrid by playing a blinder. Ruud continues to scare the living daylights out of every defence and could have settled the game before half-time but for a couple of rare misses.

As the clock ticked on, the tension levels rose, but as Eric Cantona said recently: "United have mental strength."

We continued to create chances and then Ryan Giggs gave Paul Scholes an opportunity. With the kind of form Scholesy has shown recently, a goal was inevitable. 1–0.

Stress disappeared from the players and fans alike and just before the final whistle Ruud put the result beyond doubt.

"We want our trophy back," the Reds sang. One win of the remaining three that would see us crowned as Champions again was out of the way. Two to go. Please let it be so. **BC**

> "We had to keep our nerve today. You start to wonder what kind of day it will be. Patience was required"
>
> SIR ALEX FERGUSON

Manchester United
BECKHAM (11), VAN NISTELROOY 3 (32, 37, 53)

4

Charlton Athletic
JENSEN (13)

1

SAT 3 MAY 03 ◆ 12.30PM ◆ OLD TRAFFORD ◆ ATT: 67,721 ◆ FA PREMIERSHIP ◆ REFEREE: M HALSEY ◆ ENTERTAINMENT:: ❍❍❍❍❍

Another vital game, another Ruud goal (or three!)

They think it's all over...

WHEN DENIS LAW SET THE MANCHESTER UNITED CLUB SCORING RECORD OF 46 GOALS IN A SEASON MANY THOUGHT IT WOULD STAND FOR ALL TIME. THAT RUUD VAN NISTELROOY, A PLAYER WHOSE CAREER WAS ALMOST OVER JUST THREE YEARS AGO, HAS GOT TO WITHIN TOUCHING DISTANCE OF THAT GREAT MILESTONE IS A TRULY AMAZING ACHIEVEMENT.

TODAY THE FLYING DUTCHMAN gave yet another of those complete striker performances we've become familiar with, and in powering United towards the title emphasised yet again the folly of handing out Player of the Year awards well before the season's end.

100 BY WINNING THIS ONE, UNITED CLINCHED A 100% SUCCESS RATE AGAINST LONDON CLUBS AT OLD TRAFFORD IN 2002/03

United's first was scored by Real Madrid's David Beckham – except he doesn't play for Real Madrid and (probably) never will. Nonetheless, the most talked about non-transfer target in history got the Reds off to a good start.

But just when United fans were

showing a cockiness more befitting their title rivals down south, Roy Carroll's hasty clearance from Roy Keane's ill-judged backpass gifted Charlton an equaliser. Carroll's mis-kick bobbled as far as Claus Jensen who cooly chipped the ball into the unguarded net from 30 yards.

For a short period, nervous looks were exchanged in the stands, though none on a par with those fraught minutes before Paul Scholes' goal at White Hart Lane last weekend. And any slight cause for concern vanished when the Van

The Premiership trophy is in sight

> "The greatest compliment I can pay Ruud is that he is on his way to becoming one of the greatest strikers of all-time"
>
> SIR ALEX FERGUSON

Nistelrooy show rolled into town.

A lightning fast swivel and smartly taken shot for the first was bettered by an exquisite lob for the second. The game was over by half-time and the Dutch striker's inevitable hat-trick came with a superbly taken second-half finish in front of his adoring followers in the Stretford End.

David Beckham had a blinder, while Roy Keane was again impeccable in the centre of midfield, just weeks after being written off as a spent force.

But people never seem to learn with Manchester United. All season long pundits have been falling over themselves to decree the end of the United 'dynasty' and Arsenal whooped it up like an American going into Baghdad, while United quietly got on with the job in hand. The Reds know the dance all too well and with it looking likely that the country would again be forced to eat its words, thousands headed into Manchester city centre to celebrate. Cheers Ruud! **TH**

Everton CAMPBELL (8)

1

Manchester United BECKHAM (43), VAN NISTELROOY (79 PEN)

2

SUN 11 MAY 2003 ◆ 3PM ◆ GOODISON PARK ◆ ATT: 40,168 ◆ FA PREMIERSHIP ◆ REFEREE: M RILEY ◆ ENTERTAINMENT:: ◗◗◗◗◗

Scholesy looks worried, but Ruud calmly rolls in his 44th goal of the season from the penalty spot

The champions sign off in style

WEEKS BEFORE THE FINAL GAME OF THE SEASON AT GOODISON, MOST ANTICIPATED THE NERVY PROSPECT OF UNITED GOING TO MERSEYSIDE NEEDING VICTORY.

WHILE UNITED HAVE INDULGED IN weekly bouts of transcendent entertainment, though, the efforts of Bolton and Leeds in stalling Arsenal contrived to see us crowned champions a week earlier. Relaxed in that pleasant knowledge, 3,000 Reds (that's the official estimate, though it seemed a lot more) made the short trip in celebratory mood.

United's usual medley of anti-Scouse songs coupled with a flag bearing the message 'The only time the Premiership will be won on Merseyside' hardly endeared the Reds to the home fans. Nevertheless, Evertonians were still honourable enough to applaud injured Wes Brown as he was carried around the pitch on a stretcher. This despite the realisation that their team would be cruelly dropping out of the top six

for the first time since November and consequently would miss out on a coveted UEFA Cup spot.

They'd even seen their team go ahead with an eighth minute Campbell header, but despite Wayne Rooney having three clear scoring chances, it was United who dominated after that with some strutting play and twice as many efforts on goal.

A wondrous Beckham free-kick (amazingly his first from a dead ball in the Premiership this season) bamboozled Everton keeper Richard

UNITED AVOIDED CONCEDING A WAYNE ROONEY GOAL IN TWO GAMES v EVERTON DESPITE THE TEENAGER ATTEMPTING SEVEN SHOTS

7

"Nice one, Becks": Roy hails another Beckham free-kick special

MATCH STATS

EVERTON		MANCHESTER UNITED
45%	POSSESSION	55%
5	SHOTS ON TARGET	10
7	SHOTS OFF TARGET	11
6	CORNERS	6
17	FOULS CONCEDED	16
5	BOOKINGS	3
0	RED CARDS	0

United star man ★

Ryan Giggs Finishing the season in style

MINUTES	90
GOALS	0
SHOTS	1
PASSES	52
PASS COMPLETION %	77%
CROSSES	10
DRIBBLES	13
DRIBBLE SUCCESS %	62%

What the papers said...

'The scenes of real jubilation and almost tearful triumph that greeted this wonderful success showed just how much the defeat of Arsenal in the title race meant to the United team.'
David Maddock, Daily Mirror

'Sir Alex Ferguson had a smile as wide as the nearby River Mersey at Goodison Park last night while his troops celebrated their eighth title triumph in 11 stunning years.'
Kevin Francis, Daily Star

'Like true champions Manchester United kept going right to the end, coming from behind to deny Everton a Uefa Cup place. Ruud van Nistelrooy's 25th Premiership goal of the season sealed victory, as well as the Golden Boot as the division's top scorer, and if the decisive penalty award was questionable, there was no doubting United's superiority.'
Phil Shaw, The Independent

Wright to level the score two minutes before half-time. And Everton's frustration was complete in the 79th minute when ref Mike Riley awarded a soft penalty after Stubbs had a gentle tug at Ruud Van Nistelrooy. Naturally, the Dutchman converted the spot-kick, a goal that lifted his total to 44 for the season and confirmed him as the Premiership's Golden Boot winner with 25 goals.

The United fans applauded the disappointed Everton players at the final whistle, prior to the presentation of the Premiership trophy in front of the travelling contingent. Then the celebrations began in earnest as the players illustrated their unbridled joy by joining in terrace anthems like "We've got our trophy back" and "Champions".

Just when they seemed finished and the applause was ringing out for one last time, Van Nistelrooy ran back across the field and, ignoring a policeman, whipped his shirt off and threw it into the United end. Happy days. **AM**

> "We've been beaten by a brilliant free-kick and a soft penalty"
>
> DAVID MOYES

CHAPTER SEVEN

Stat Attack! ALL THE VITAL FACTS AND FIGURES FROM A THRILLING SEASON…

Opta @ PLANETFOOTBALL.com

Month	Date	H/A	Opposition	Result*	Starting Line-up	Substitutes Used
AUGUST	Weds 14	A	Zalaegerszeg TE (CL Qualifier)	0–1	Carroll Silvestre Blanc O'Shea Brown Beckham Keane Veron Giggs Solskjaer Van Nistelrooy	P Neville Forlan
	Sat 17	H	West Bromwich Albion	1–0	Carroll Silvestre Blanc O'Shea P Neville Beckham Keane Butt Veron Giggs Van Nistelrooy	Solskjaer• Scholes Forlan
	Fri 23	A	Chelsea	2–2	Carroll Silvestre Blanc O'Shea P Neville Beckham• Keane Butt Scholes Giggs• Van Nistelrooy	Solskjaer Veron Forlan
	Tues 27	H	Zalaegerszeg TE (CL Qualifier)	5–0	Carroll Silvestre Blanc Ferdinand P Neville Beckham• Keane Veron Scholes• Giggs Van Nistelrooy••	Solskjaer• O'Shea Forlan
	Sat 31	A	Sunderland	1–1	Carroll Silvestre Blanc Ferdinand P Neville Beckham Keane Veron Giggs• Solskjaer Van Nistelrooy	O'Shea Forlan
SEPTEMBER	Tues 3	H	Middlesbrough	1–0	Barthez Silvestre Blanc Ferdinand P Neville Beckham Butt Veron Giggs Scholes Van Nistelrooy•	Solskjaer Forlan O'Shea
	Weds 11	A	Bolton Wanderers	0–1	Barthez Silvestre Blanc Ferdinand P Neville Beckham Butt Veron Giggs Solskjaer Van Nistelrooy	Forlan
	Sat 14	A	Leeds United	0–1	Barthez Silvestre Blanc Ferdinand O'Shea Beckham Butt P Neville Giggs Solskjaer Van Nistelrooy	Fortune Forlan
	Weds 18	H	Maccabi Haifa (CL stage 1)	5–2	Barthez Silvestre Blanc Ferdinand O'Shea Beckham P Neville Veron• Giggs Solskjaer• Van Nistelrooy•	Forlan• Ricardo Pugh
	Sat 21	H	Tottenham Hotspur	1–0	Barthez Silvestre O'Shea Ferdinand P Neville Beckham Butt Veron Giggs Solskjaer Van Nistelrooy•	Forlan G Neville Pugh
	Tues 24	A	Bayer Leverkusen (CL stage 1)	2–1	Barthez Silvestre Blanc Ferdinand O'Shea Beckham Butt Veron P Neville Giggs Van Nistelrooy•	G Neville Forlan Solskjaer
	Sat 28	A	Charlton Athletic	3–1	Barthez O'Shea Blanc Ferdinand P Neville Beckham Butt Forlan Giggs• Scholes• Solskjaer	G Neville Van Nistelrooy•
OCTOBER	Tues 1	H	Olympiakos (CL stage 1)	4–0	Barthez Silvestre Blanc Ferdinand G Neville Beckham Butt Veron• Giggs•• Solskjaer• Scholes	O'Shea Fortune Forlan
	Mon 7	A	Everton	3–0	Barthez Silvestre Blanc O'Shea G Neville Beckham Butt Veron Scholes•• Giggs Van Nistelrooy•	Solskjaer Forlan P Neville
	Sat 19	A	Fulham	1–1	Barthez Silvestre Blanc O'Shea G Neville Beckham P Neville Veron Giggs Scholes Solskjaer•	Fortune Forlan
	Weds 23	H	Olympiakos (CL stage 1)	3–2	Barthez Silvestre Blanc• O'Shea Beckham P Neville Veron• Scholes• Giggs Forlan	Fortune Chadwick Richardson
	Sat 26	A	Aston Villa	1–1	Barthez Silvestre Blanc Ferdinand Beckham P Neville Veron Scholes. Solskjaer Forlan•	Fortune
NOVEMBER	Tues 29	A	Maccabi Haifa (CL stage 1)	0–3	Ricardo Silvestre O'Shea Ferdinand G Neville Solskjaer P Neville Fortune Richardson Scholes Forlan	Nardiello Timm
	Sat 2	H	Southampton	2–1	Barthez Silvestre Blanc Ferdinand G Neville Beckham P Neville• Veron Giggs Scholes Van Nistelrooy	Solskjaer Forlan• O'Shea
	Weds 6	H	Leicester City (Worth'ton Cup 3)	2–0	Carroll O'Shea May Ferdinand G Neville Beckham• P Neville Forlan Fortune Solskjaer Nardiello	Scholes Veron Richardson•
	Sat 9	H	Manchester City	1–3	Barthez Silvestre Blanc Ferdinand G Neville Scholes P Neville Veron Giggs Solskjaer• Van Nistelrooy	Forlan O'Shea
	Weds 13	H	Bayer Leverkusen (CL stage 1)	2–0	Ricardo Silvestre Blanc Ferdinand O'Shea Beckham Fortune Veron• Giggs Scholes Van Nistelrooy•	G Neville Solskjaer Chadwick
	Sun 17	A	West Ham United	1–1	Barthez Silvestre Blanc Brown O'Shea Scholes Fortune Veron Giggs Solskjaer Van Nistelrooy•	Forlan O'Shea
	Sat 23	H	Newcastle United	5–3	Barthez Silvestre Blanc Brown O'Shea Scholes• Fortune Solskjaer• Giggs Forlan Van Nistelrooy•••	Richardson Roche Veron
DECEMBER	Tues 26	H	FC Basel (CL stage 2)	3–1	Barthez Silvestre O'Shea Brown G Neville Solskjaer• Fortune Veron Scholes Giggs Van Nistelrooy••	Forlan May Chadwick
	Sun 1	A	Liverpool	2–1	Barthez Silvestre O'Shea Brown P Neville Scholes Fortune Solskjaer Giggs Forlan•• Van Nistelrooy	P Neville May Stewart
	Weds 4	H	Burnley (Worthington Cup 4)	2–0	Carroll Silvestre May Brown P Neville Stewart O'Shea Pugh Chadwick Forlan• Van Nistelrooy	Solskjaer• Giggs Scholes
	Sat 7	A	Arsenal	2–0	Barthez Silvestre Blanc Brown G Neville Solskjaer Keane Veron• Giggs Scholes• Van Nistelrooy	Forlan
	Weds 11	H	Deportivo (CL stage 2)	2–0	Barthez Silvestre Blanc Brown O'Shea Solskjaer P Neville Keane Giggs Scholes Van Nistelrooy••	Beckham Forlan Richardson
	Sat 14	H	West Ham United	3–0	Barthez Silvestre O'Shea Brown G Neville Solskjaer• P Neville Veron• Giggs Scholes Van Nistelrooy	Beckham Forlan Blanc
	Tues 17	H	Chelsea (Worth'ton Cup 5)	1–0	Barthez Silvestre O'Shea Brown G Neville Beckham P Neville Veron Giggs Scholes Forlan•	
	Sun 22	A	Blackburn Rovers	0–1	Barthez Silvestre O'Shea Brown G Neville Solskjaer P Neville Scholes Giggs Forlan Van Nistelrooy	Keane Beckham Blanc
	Thurs 26	A	Middlesbrough	1–3	Barthez O'Shea Blanc Brown G Neville Solskjaer Keane Veron Giggs• Scholes Van Nistelrooy	Beckham Ferdinand
	Sat 28	H	Birmingham City	2–0	Barthez Silvestre Ferdinand Brown O'Shea Beckham• Keane Veron Solskjaer Scholes Forlan•	Richardson P Neville Giggs
JANUARY	Weds 1	H	Sunderland	2–1	Barthez Silvestre Ferdinand Brown O'Shea Beckham Keane Veron Solskjaer Scholes Forlan	Carroll Giggs G Neville
	Sat 4	H	Portsmouth (FA Cup 3)	4–1	Carroll Silvestre Ferdinand Blanc G Neville Beckham• Keane P Neville Richardson Giggs Van Nistelrooy••	Stewart Scholes• Brown
	Tues 7	H	Blackburn (Worth'ton Cup SF 1)	1–1	Barthez Silvestre Ferdinand Brown G Neville Beckham P Neville Keane Scholes• Giggs Van Nistelrooy•	Solskjaer Forlan
	Sat 11	A	West Bromwich Albion	3–1	Barthez Silvestre Ferdinand Brown G Neville Beckham P Neville Solskjaer• Scholes• Van Nistelrooy•	Forlan O'Shea
	Sat 18	H	Chelsea	2–1	Barthez Silvestre Ferdinand Brown G Neville Beckham P Neville Solskjaer Scholes• Van Nistelrooy•	Forlan• Giggs Veron
	Weds 22	A	Blackburn (Worth'ton Cup SF 2)	3–1	Barthez Silvestre Ferdinand Brown G Neville Beckham Keane Veron Giggs Scholes•• Van Nistelrooy•	Butt Forlan
	Sun 26	H	West Ham United (FA Cup 4)	6–0	Barthez P Neville• Ferdinand O'Shea G Neville Beckham Keane Veron Giggs•• Scholes Van Nistelrooy••	Butt Forlan Solskjaer•
	Sat 1	H	Southampton	2–0	Barthez Silvestre Ferdinand O'Shea G Neville Beckham Keane Veron Giggs• Scholes Van Nistelrooy	Carroll Scholes Forlan
	Tues 4	A	Birmingham City	1–0	Carroll Silvestre Ferdinand Brown G Neville Beckham Keane Veron Giggs Scholes Van Nistelrooy•	Solskjaer
FEBRUARY	Sun 9	H	Manchester City	1–1	Carroll Silvestre Ferdinand Brown G Neville Beckham Keane Veron Giggs Scholes Van Nistelrooy•	Butt Solskjaer
	Sat 15	A	Arsenal (FA Cup 5)	0–2	Barthez Silvestre Ferdinand Brown G Neville Beckham Keane Scholes Solskjaer Giggs Van Nistelrooy	Forlan Butt
	Weds 19	H	Juventus (CL stage 2)	2–1	Barthez Silvestre Ferdinand Brown• G Neville Beckham Keane Butt Giggs Scholes Van Nistelrooy•	O'Shea Solskjaer Forlan
	Sat 22	A	Bolton Wanderers	1–1	Barthez O'Shea Ferdinand Brown G Neville Beckham Keane Veron Giggs Solskjaer• Van Nistelrooy•	Forlan P Neville Butt
	Tues 25	A	Juventus (CL stage 2)	3–0	Barthez O'Shea Ferdinand Keane G Neville Beckham P Neville Butt Veron Solskjaer Forlan	Giggs•• Pugh Van Nistelrooy•
	Sun 2	N	Liverpool (Worth'ton Cup final)	0–2	Barthez Silvestre Ferdinand Keane G Neville Beckham Keane Veron Giggs Scholes Van Nistelrooy	Solskjaer
MARCH	Weds 5	H	Leeds United	2–1	Barthez Silvestre• Ferdinand Keane O'Shea Beckham Butt Veron Fortune Scholes Van Nistelrooy	P Neville Giggs G Neville
	Weds 12	H	FC Basel (CL stage 2)	1–1	Carroll O'Shea Ferdinand Blanc G Neville• Fletcher P Neville Butt Richardson Solskjaer Forlan	Giggs Beckham Scholes
	Sat 15	H	Aston Villa	1–0	Barthez Silvestre Ferdinand O'Shea G Neville Beckham• Butt Scholes Giggs Solskjaer Van Nistelrooy	
	Tues 18	A	Deportivo (CL stage 2)	0–2	Ricardo Roche Blanc O'Shea Lynch Fletcher P Neville Butt Pugh Forlan Giggs	Stewart Webber Richardson
	Sat 22	H	Fulham	3–0	Barthez O'Shea Ferdinand Brown G Neville Beckham Scholes Butt Giggs Solskjaer Van Nistelrooy•••	
APRIL	Sat 5	A	Liverpool	4–0	Barthez Silvestre Ferdinand Brown G Neville Solskjaer• Keane P Neville Giggs• Scholes Van Nistelrooy	O'Shea Beckham Butt
	Tues 8	H	Real Madrid (CL QF 1)	1–3	Barthez Silvestre Ferdinand Brown G Neville Beckham Keane Butt Veron Giggs Van Nistelrooy•	O'Shea Solskjaer
	Sat 12	A	Newcastle United	6–2	Barthez O'Shea Ferdinand Silvestre Brown Solskjaer• Keane Butt Giggs• Scholes••• Van Nistelrooy	Forlan G Neville Blanc
	Weds 16	H	Arsenal	2–2	Barthez O'Shea Ferdinand Silvestre Brown Solskjaer Keane Butt Scholes Giggs• Van Nistelrooy	G Neville
	Sat 19	H	Blackburn	3–1	Barthez P Neville Ferdinand Silvestre Brown Beckham Fortune Butt Giggs Scholes•• Van Nistelrooy	Ricardo Keane Solskjaer
	Weds 23	H	Real Madrid (CL QF 2)	4–3	Barthez O'Shea Ferdinand Silvestre Brown Solskjaer Keane Butt Veron Giggs Van Nistelrooy•	Beckham•• P Neville Fortune
	Sun 27	A	Tottenham Hotspur	2–0	Carroll O'Shea Ferdinand Silvestre Brown Beckham Keane Scholes• Solskjaer Giggs Van Nistelrooy•	G Neville Fortune
MAY	Sat 3	A	Charlton Athletic	4–1	Carroll O'Shea Ferdinand Silvestre Brown Beckham• Keane Scholes Solskjaer Giggs Van Nistelrooy•••	Veron Butt Forlan
	Sun 11	A	Everton	2–1	Carroll O'Shea Ferdinand Silvestre Brown Beckham• Keane Scholes Solskjaer Giggs Van Nistelrooy•	Blanc P Neville Fortune

* United's score is given first in every case • Goal scored

Manchester United squad 2002/03

 1 FABIEN BARTHEZ
Premiership: 30 (0) apps, 0 goals
FA Cup: 2 (0) apps, 0 goals
League Cup: 4 (0) apps, 0 goals
Champions League: 10 (0) apps,
0 goals TOTAL: 46 apps, 0 goals

 2 GARY NEVILLE
Premiership: 19 (7) apps, 0 goals
FA Cup: 2 (0) apps, 0 goals
League Cup: 5 (0) apps, 0 goals
Champs League: 8 (2) apps, 1 goal
TOTAL: 35 (9) apps, 0 goals

 3 PHIL NEVILLE
Premiership: 19 (6) apps, 1 goal
FA Cup: 2 (0) apps, 1 goal
League Cup: 4 (0) apps, 0 goals
Champs League: 10 (2) apps, 0
goals TOTAL: 35 (8) apps, 2 goals

 4 SEBA VERON
Premiership: 21 (4) apps, 2 goals
FA Cup: 1 (0) apps, 0 goals
League Cup: 4 (1) apps, 0 goals
Champs League: 11 (0) apps, 4
goals TOTAL: 37 (5) apps, 6 goals

 5 LAURENT BLANC
Premiership: 15 (4) apps, 0 goals
FA Cup: 1 (0) apps, 0 goals
League Cup: 0 (0) apps, 0 goals
Champs League: 9 (0) apps, 1 goal
TOTAL: 25 (4) apps, 1 goal

 6 RIO FERDINAND
Premiership: 27 (1) apps, 0 goals
FA Cup: 3 (0) apps, 0 goals
League Cup: 4 (0) apps, 0 goals
Champs League: 11 (0) apps, 0 goals
TOTAL: 45 (1) apps, 0 goals

 7 DAVID BECKHAM
Premiership: 27 (4) apps, 6 goals
FA Cup: 3 (0) apps, 1 goal
League Cup: 5 (0) apps, 1 goal
Champs Lge: 10 (3) apps, 3 goals
TOTAL: 45 (7) apps, 11 goals

 8 NICKY BUTT
Premiership: 14 (4) apps, 0 goals
FA Cup: 0 (0) apps, 0 goals
League Cup: 0 (0) apps, 0 goals
Champions League: 8 (0) apps, 0 goals
TOTAL: 22 (7) apps, 0 goals

 9 VACANT NUMBER

 10 RUUD v NISTELROOY
Premiership: 33 (1) apps, 25 goals
FA Cup: 3 (0) apps, 4 goals
League Cup: 4 (0) apps, 1 goal
Champs Lge: 10 (1) apps, 14 goals
TOTAL: 50 (2) apps, 44 goals

 11 RYAN GIGGS
Premiership: 32 (4) apps, 8 goals
FA Cup: 3 (0) apps, 2 goals
League Cup: 4 (1) apps, 0 goals
Champs Lge: 13 (3) apps, 5 goals
TOTAL: 52 (7) apps, 15 goals

 13 ROY CARROLL
Premiership: 8 (2) apps, 0 goals
FA Cup: 1 (0) apps, 0 goals
League Cup: 2 (0) apps, 0 goals
Champions League: 3 (0) apps, 0 goals
TOTAL: 14 (2) apps, 0 goals

 14 DAVID MAY
Premiership: 0 (1) apps, 0 goals
FA Cup: 0 (0) apps, 0 goals
League Cup: 2 (0) apps, 0 goals
Champs League: 0 (1) apps, 0 goals
TOTAL: 0 (2) apps, 0 goals

 15 LUKE CHADWICK
Premiership: 0 (1) apps, 0 goals
FA Cup: 0 (0) apps, 0 goals
League Cup: 1 (0) apps, 0 goals
Champs League: 0 (3) apps, 0 goals
TOTAL: 1 (4) apps, 0 goals

 16 ROY KEANE
Premiership: 19 (2) apps, 0 goals
FA Cup: 3 (0) apps, 0 goals
League Cup: 2 (0) apps, 0 goals
Champs League: 6 (0) apps, 0 goals
TOTAL: 30 (2) apps, 0 goals

 17 MICHAEL STEWART
Premiership: 0 (1) apps, 0 goals
FA Cup: 0 (1) apps, 0 goals
League Cup: 1 (0) apps, 0 goals
Champs League: 0 (1) apps, 0 goals
TOTAL: 1 (3) apps, 0 goals

 18 PAUL SCHOLES
Premiership: 31 (2) apps, 14 goals
FA Cup: 2 (1) apps, 1 goal
League Cup: 4 (2) apps, 3 goals
Champs League: 9 (1) apps, 2 goals
TOTAL: 46 (6) apps, 20 goals

 19 RICARDO
Premiership: 0 (1) apps, 0 goals
FA Cup: 0 (0) apps, 0 goals
League Cup: 0 (0) apps, 0 goals
Champs League: 3 (1) apps, 0 goals
TOTAL: 3 (2) apps, 0 goals

 20 OLE SOLSKJAER
Premiership: 29 (8) apps, 9 goals
FA Cup: 1 (1) apps, 1 goal
League Cup: 1 (3) apps, 1 goal
Champs League: 9 (5) apps, 4 goals
TOTAL: 40(17) apps, 15 goals

 21 DIEGO FORLAN
Premiership: 7 (18) apps, 6 goals
FA Cup: 0 (2) apps, 0 goals
League Cup: 3 (2) apps, 2 goals
Champs League: 5 (9) apps, 1 goal
TOTAL: 15 (30) apps, 9 goals

 22 JOHN O'SHEA
Premiership: 26 (6) apps, 0 goals
FA Cup: 1 (0) apps, 0 goals
League Cup: 3 (0) apps, 0 goals
Champs League: 12 (4) apps, 0
goalsTOTAL: 42 (10) apps, 0 goals

 23 BOJAN DJORDJIC
Did not play

 24 WES BROWN
Premiership: 22 (0) apps, 0 goals
FA Cup: 1 (1) apps, 0 goals
League Cup: 5 (0) apps, 0 goals
Champs League: 6 (0) apps, 1 goal
TOTAL: 34 (1) apps, 1 goal

 25 QUINTON FORTUNE
Premiership: 5 (4) apps, 0 goals
FA Cup: 0 (0) apps, 0 goals
League Cup: 1 (0) apps, 0 goals
Champs League: 3 (3) apps, 0 goals
TOTAL: 9 (7) apps, 0 goals

 26 DANNY PUGH
Premiership: 0 (1) apps, 0 goals
FA Cup: 0 (0) apps, 0 goals
League Cup: 1 (0) apps, 0 goals
Champs League: 1 (2) apps, 0 goals
TOTAL: 2 (3) apps, 0 goals

 27 MIKAEL SILVESTRE
Premiership: 34 (0) apps, 1 goal
FA Cup: 2 (0) apps, 0 goals
League Cup: 5 (0) apps, 0 goals
Champs League: 13 (0) apps, 0
goalsTOTAL: 54 (0) apps, 1 goal

 28 KIRK HILTON
Did not play

29 VACANT NUMBER

 30 BEN WILLIAMS
Did not play

 31 DARREN FLETCHER
Premiership: 0 (0) apps, 0 goals
FA Cup: 0 (0) apps, 0 goals
League Cup: 0 (0) apps, 0 goals
Champs League: 2 (0) apps, 0 goals
TOTAL: 2 (0) apps, 0 goals

32 VACANT NUMBER

33 VACANT NUMBER

 34 LEE ROCHE
Premiership: 0 (1) apps, 0 goals
FA Cup: 0 (0) apps, 0 goals
League Cup: 0 (0) apps, 0 goals
Champs League: 1 (0) apps, 0 goals
TOTAL: 1 (1) apps, 0 goals

35 VACANT NUMBER

 36 JIMMY DAVIS
Did not play

 37 DANNY WEBBER
Premiership: 0 (0) apps, 0 goals
FA Cup: 0 (0) apps, 0 goals
League Cup: 0 (0) apps, 0 goals
Champs League: 0 (1) apps, 0 goals
TOTAL: 0 (1) apps, 0 goals

 38 MARK LYNCH
Premiership: 0 (0) apps, 0 goals
FA Cup: 0 (0) apps, 0 goals
League Cup: 0 (0) apps, 0 goals
Champs League: 1 (0) apps, 0 goals
TOTAL: 1 (0) apps, 0 goals

 39 PAUL TIERNEY
Did not play

 40 DANIEL NARDIELLO
Premiership: 0 (0) apps, 0 goals
FA Cup: 0 (0) apps, 0 goals
League Cup: 1 (0) apps, 0 goals
Champs League: 0 (1) apps, 0 goals
TOTAL: 1 (1) apps, 0 goals

 41 ALAN TATE
Did not play

 42 KIERAN RICHARDSON
Premiership: 0 (2) apps, 0 goals
FA Cup: 1 (0) apps, 0 goals
League Cup: 0 (1) apps, 0 goals
Champs League: 2 (3) apps, 0 goals
TOTAL: 3 (6) apps, 1 goal

43 MADS TIMM
Premiership: 0 (0) apps, 0 goals
FA Cup: 0 (0) apps, 0 goals
League Cup: 0 (0) apps, 0 goals
Champs League: 0 (1) apps, 0 goals
TOTAL: 0 (1) apps, 0 goals

44 LUKE STEELE
Did not play

45 VACANT NUMBER

Substitute appearances in brackets

FA BARCLAYCARD PREMIERSHIP TABLE 2002/03

	P	W	D	L	F	A	PTS
MANCHESTER UTD	38	25	8	5	74	34	**83**
ARSENAL	38	23	9	6	85	42	78
NEWCASTLE UNITED	38	21	6	11	63	48	69
CHELSEA	38	19	10	9	68	38	67
LIVERPOOL	38	18	10	10	61	41	64
BLACKBURN	38	16	12	10	52	43	60
EVERTON	38	17	8	13	48	49	59
SOUTHAMPTON	38	13	13	12	43	46	54
MANCHESTER CITY	38	15	6	17	47	54	51
TOTTENHAM HOTSPUR	38	14	8	16	51	62	50
MIDDLESBROUGH	38	13	10	15	48	44	49
CHARLTON	38	14	7	17	45	56	49
BIRMINGHAM CITY	38	13	9	16	41	49	48
FULHAM	38	13	9	16	41	50	48
LEEDS UNITED	38	14	5	19	58	57	47
ASTON VILLA	38	12	9	17	42	47	45
BOLTON WANDERERS	38	10	14	14	41	51	44
WEST HAM UNITED	38	10	12	16	42	59	42
WEST BROMICH ALBION	38	6	8	24	29	65	26
SUNDERLAND	38	4	7	24	21	65	19

The BEST v the REST

Find out where United stars stand in the Opta rankings based on statistical analysis of every save, pass, tackle and shot during the 2002/03 Premiership season...

GOALKEEPERS

1	BRAD FRIEDEL	BLACKBURN ROVERS
2	SHAY GIVEN	NEWCASTLE UNITED
3	RICHARD WRIGHT	EVERTON
4	KASEY KELLER	TOTTENHAM HOTSPUR
5	PETER SCHMEICHEL	MANCHESTER CITY
15	**FABIEN BARTHEZ**	**MANCHESTER UNITED**

DEFENDERS

1	SAMI HYYPIA	LIVERPOOL
2	JONATHAN WOODGATE	NEWCASTLE UNITED
3	MARCEL DESAILLY	CHELSEA
4	**MIKAEL SILVESTRE**	**MANCHESTER UNITED**
5	**RIO FERDINAND**	**MANCHESTER UNITED**

MIDFIELDERS

1	PATRICK VIEIRA	ARSENAL
2	**ROY KEANE**	**MANCHESTER UNITED**
3	DIETMAR HAMANN	LIVERPOOL
4	FRANK LAMPARD	CHELSEA
5	STEVEN GERRARD	LIVERPOOL

ATTACKING MIDFIELDERS

1	ROBERT PIRES	ARSENAL
2	**PAUL SCHOLES**	**MANCHESTER UNITED**
3	DAVID THOMPSON	BLACKBURN ROVERS
4	**DAVID BECKHAM**	**MANCHESTER UNITED**
5	HARRY KEWELL	LEEDS UNITED

STRIKERS

1	THIERRY HENRY	ARSENAL
2	**RUUD VAN NISTELROOY**	**MANCHESTER UNITED**
3	MARK VIDUKA	LEEDS UNITED
4	JAMES BEATTIE	SOUTHAMPTON
5	GIANFRANCO ZOLA	CHELSEA

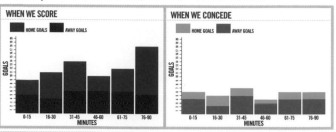

When, Where and How? 2002/03 PREMIERSHIP STATS ONLY

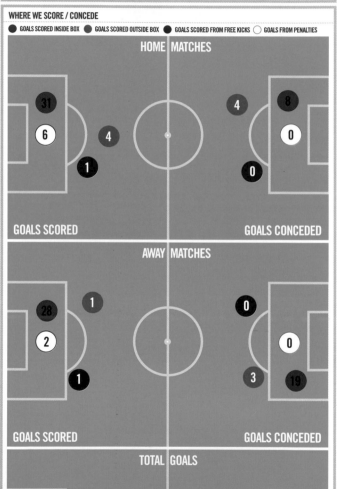

United Top of the League!

The best team always finishes on top of the Premiership and here's some of the reasons why United are number one...

MOST SUCCESSFUL PASSES	
Manchester United	13,797
Arsenal	12,965
Chelsea	12,209
Liverpool	11,743
Newcastle United	11,519

MOST SHOTS ATTEMPTED	
Manchester United	470
Aston Villa	470
Chelsea	461
Liverpool	456
Arsenal	444

MOST GOALS INSIDE BOX	
Manchester United	64
Arsenal	59
Chelsea	51
Liverpool	50
Leeds United	44

MOST CROSSES ATTEMPTED	
Manchester United	1038
Aston Villa	1029
Everton	966
Sunderland	953
Newcastle United	940

United Player of the Year 2002/03 *

RUUD VAN NISTELROOY

■ Ruud took eight penalties in the Premiership - the most by a single player. He scored them all.

■ Hotshot Ruud averaged a shot every 29 minutes in the Premiership.

■ 100 per cent of Ruud's Premiership goals came from inside the penalty area.

■ 45 per cent of Ruud's shots found the back of the net (18 shots, 10 goals) in the group phases of the Champions League. No striker in Europe could match this incredible goals-to-shots ratio.

* as voted for by the readers of UNITED magazine

United Young Player of the Year 2002/03 *

JOHN O'SHEA

■ John was the only United player out of 31 used in Europe to appear in all 16 of United's Champions League matches.

■ John played in 52 of United's 63 league and cup matches in 2002/03. Only three players – Ryan Giggs, Mikael Silvestre and Ole Solskjaer – appeared in more.

■ 30 per cent of O'Shea's 54 crosses found their target – only Seba Veron was more accurate.

■ Sheasy won 84 per cent of his tackles in Premiership games. Rio Ferdinand was the only United star to win more.

* as voted for by the readers of UNITED magazine

THE TOP UNITED PERFORMERS 2002/03

SHOTS ON TARGET
V NISTELROOY	60
SOLSKJAER	32
GIGGS	29
SCHOLES	29
BECKHAM	27

GOALS TO SHOTS %
V NISTELROOY	25%
SCHOLES	20%
FORLAN	18%
GIGGS	16%
SOLSKJAER	14%

MOST PASSES
SCHOLES	1629
SILVESTRE	1578
BECKHAM	1531
VERON	1497
KEANE	1422

PASSING ACCURACY
KEANE	89%
FORTUNE	86%
NEVILLE	85%
BLANC	84%
SCHOLES	82%

GOAL ASSISTS
GIGGS	11
BECKHAM	8
SILVESTRE	7
SOLSKJAER	6
G. NEVILLE	4
V NISTELROOY	4

MOST DRIBBLES
GIGGS	217
V NISTELROOY	136
BECKHAM	125
SILVESTRE	122
SCHOLES	112

MOST CROSSES
BECKHAM	363
GIGGS	200
SOLSKJAER	97
SILVESTRE	91
G. NEVILLE	77

CROSSING ACCURACY
VERON	31%
O'SHEA	30%
G. NEVILLE	27%
BECKHAM	25%
GIGGS	22%

MOST TACKLES
SILVESTRE	106
KEANE	84
SCHOLES	77
BECKHAM	76
O'SHEA	74

TACKLE SUCCESS
FERDINAND	86%
O'SHEA	84%
SILVESTRE	81%
BUTT	79%
BROWN	74%

INTERCEPTIONS
SILVESTRE	23
FERDINAND	21
BLANC	19
SCHOLES	17
KEANE	15

CHAPTER EIGHT

LET'S CELEBR-EIGHT!

AFTER A TUMULTUOUS SEASON OF SOARING HIGHS AND
CRUSHING LOWS, THE LADS CAME THROUGH TO WIN
THE TITLE. AND THEY MADE SURE THEY CELEBRATED
OUR EIGHTH PREMIERSHIP SUCCESS IN STYLE...

"It makes me feel proud to have equalled the record of winning eight championship medals. Now, hopefully, I can go on and win as many as I can and put myself out of sight!

"I've also passed a couple of other landmarks in scoring my 100th goal for the club and passing 500 appearances. What with becoming a father as well, it has been a really great year for me.

"For pure ability and talent, player for player, this is the best United team I've played in. And it can get better. We are champions now and that gives you an extra bit of confidence."

RYAN GIGGS

"We've worked so hard and we all deserved this success. It is a great double celebration for me. To win the Premiership and get the Golden Boot makes it all so special. Last year, I won some individual awards but they meant nothing as the team won nothing.

"We have now though and it is a fantastic feeling. We will have a holiday and come back refreshed next year."

RUUD VAN NISTELROOY

"I'm absolutely delighted and proud of all the team. I'd like to thank Sir Alex, our coach Carlos Queiroz, all the staff and all the fans for their fantastic support this season.

"I think our new coach Carlos Queiroz had a big influence on our success this season. The fact that Carlos was very disciplined was good for the players. Even for home games, we now stay in a hotel the night before.

"The fact that we won nothing last year wasn't acceptable. You need to have a laugh and joke in training but last year I think things got too relaxed. That's why Carlos was brought in. It was time for a change."

ROY KEANE

"I came to Manchester United to win championships and be in contention to win everything we are going for. I wanted to win something this season.

"After losing in the Worthington Cup Final and the disappointment of getting knocked out of the European Cup, everything rested on the Premiership. To go out and win it before the final game is fantastic especially when you consider the position we were in halfway through the season.

"When you have confidence in your team-mates, it gives you an extra edge."

RIO FERDINAND

"I THINK THIS LEAGUE WIN IS UP THERE WITH THE BEST OF THEM. THE WAY THAT WE WON IT, THE FACT THAT WE BEAT A GREAT TEAM IN ARSENAL SHOWS THAT WE ARE THE BEST TEAM IN ENGLAND. MEDALS AREN'T HANDED OUT AT CHRISTMAS AND IF YOU WIN THE LEAGUE, IT PROVES YOU ARE THE BEST REGARDLESS OF WHAT ANYONE SAYS.

"WE WERE PLAYING UNDER IMMENSE PRESSURE TO WIN EVERY GAME AND WE HANDLED THAT SUPERBLY. EVERYONE'S VERY PROUD IN THE DRESSING ROOM. THERE'S A GREAT TEAM SPIRIT HERE AND THAT'S TAKEN US ALL THE WAY TO THE TITLE.

"PEOPLE WROTE US OFF IN MID-SEASON SAYING THIS TEAM IS FINISHED. THIS TEAM ISN'T FINISHED BY A LONG SHOT."

PHIL NEVILLE

"To become the first Argentinian to win the Premiership fills me with enormous pride. I'm delighted for the people I have worked with and were alongside me during the difficult times.

"A lot of people were saying it was all over for us at Christmas but we have shown just how solid we are as club. We stayed strong because we had an obligation to win something after finishing last season without a trophy. We are a team that must win things."

SEBA VERON

"IF ANYONE HAD TOLD ME LAST AUGUST I'D PLAY OVER 50 GAMES THIS SEASON AND GET A CHAMPIONSHIP MEDAL, I'D HAVE LAUGHED AT THEM.

"IT'S BEEN AN AMAZING SEASON FOR ME PERSONALLY AND I HAVE TO THANK ALL THE PLAYERS AND COACHES FOR THAT BECAUSE THEY'VE GIVEN ME THE CONFIDENCE TO MAKE THAT BIG STEP UP FROM THE RESERVE TEAM. I'VE REALLY ENJOYED IT, IT'S FLOWN BY. IT'S BEEN THE FASTEST SEASON EVER!"

JOHN O'SHEA

"There was one point after the derby defeat when we all thought that if we don't pick ourselves up, then the league will go away from us again. I'm sure United fans thought that and I know journalists were writing every day that Man United had lost it.

"But our pride is stung by that sort of talk. Once people started saying that about us, we all dug in and fought our way back."

DAVID BECKHAM

DON'T MISS A KICK NEXT SEASON...